GARTH TURNER'S
1997
RRSP
GUIDE

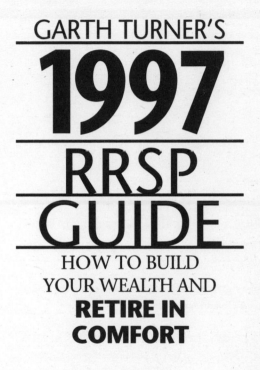

GARTH TURNER'S

1997

RRSP

GUIDE

HOW TO BUILD
YOUR WEALTH AND
RETIRE IN
COMFORT

KEY PORTER BOOKS

Canadian Cataloguing in Publication Data

Turner, Garth

Garth Turner's 1997 RRSP guide : how to build your wealth and retire in comfort

ISBN 1-55013-802-2

1. Registered Retirement Savings Plans.*   I. Title.
II. Title: 1997 RRSP guide.   III. Title: RRSP guide.

HD7129.T87 1996   332.6'042   C96-931630-5

The publisher gratefully acknowledges the assistance of the Canada Council and the the Ontario Arts Council.

The author thanks Sandra McLeod and Prashant Patel, of KPMG's Personal Advisory Services, for their meticulous attention to the technical accuracy of this book. KPMG offers, among many other services, tax and retirement planning, estate and investment planning, RRSPs and counselling on termination and employment packages.

Key Porter Books
70 The Esplanade
Toronto, Ontario
Canada M5E 1R2

Printed and bound in Canada

96 97 98 99 6 5 4 3 2 1

Contents

Introduction   **7**

Chapter 1: Big changes in 1997 rules   14
Seniors benefit   14
Contribution limits frozen until 2003   19
Carry-forward limit is eliminated   20
Administration fees are not tax-deductible   23
Investment counselling fees no longer
   tax-deductible   24
Age limit drops for RRSP contributions   25
Retiring allowance rollovers phased out   27
Getting cash from your RRSP   30

Chapter 2: The greying of Canada   32

Chapter 3: Life in the bubble   42
RRSPs: The basics at a glance   43
How much can you contribute?   52
Build your wealth by saving taxes   56
Your mortgage versus your RRSP:
   No contest   65
What kind of RRSP is right for you?   72
Ooh-la-la: Maxing your foreign content   80
How to split income with a spousal RRSP   85
Your RRSP and your real estate   89
Building your RRSP without any cash   98
Carrying forward your unused contributions   104
Should you make an overcontribution?   107
The Canadian mistake: Being
   too conservative   110
RRSPs, the sequel: Converting to a RRIF   115

**Chapter 4: What happens
if they tax RRSPs?   121**
The ability to carry forward unused
   contributions could end   122

RRSP contributions could go from tax
deductions to tax credits 122
RRSP assets could be subject
to direct taxation 123
Contribution levels could be reduced 124
The savings period could be cut 124

Chapter 5: Winning RRSP strategies 125
Invest for growth 126
Catch up on missed contributions—now 128
Contribute early 131
Maximize your cash flow 132
Load up the less-taxed spouse 133
Make the overcontribution 135
Get an interest-free loan 136
Sell yourself your own assets 137
Hold your own mortgage 138
Liberate your real estate 139
Bouchard-proof your wealth 140
Contribute now, claim it later 144
Diversify, diversify, diversify 144
Don't labour over the labour funds 149
Protect yourself from creditors 150
Tracking the common wisdom 151
Wealth without risk: Strip bonds 152
Generational strategies 158
Generation Xers 159
Baby Boomers 160
Junior Seniors 165
Senior Seniors 167

**Chapter 6: How to find an adviser
you can trust 169**

Internet resources 180
Financial advisors 180

***The Turner Report* 189**
An affordable newletter of tax and
investment strategies 191

Index 193

Introduction

Congratulations. You have just done something that puts you in an elite group: the minority of Canadians taking action to secure their financial future.

Read on. I know I can help you.

This book is about two things: hope and tools.

Contrary to what you see in the daily media, there is a great deal to be hopeful about, even if you are middle-aged and have saved next to nothing. There's hope the North American economy will do well for the next decade and a half, thanks to a winning combination of demographics, politics and corporate profits.

There is hope that low inflation and falling interest rates will create some great investment opportunities. And there's reason to hope governments will increasingly realize, and respond to, the threat an aging population poses. The 1996 federal budget certainly kick-started that process in Canada.

As for tools, we have many at our disposal—from strip bonds to mutual funds. From income-splitting to liberating your under-performing real estate. I will show you how to build wealth quickly and surely, using strategies that are always legal. With cheap rates and strong financial markets, there has rarely been a more powerful time to be an investor.

Ironically, most Canadians do not realize what opportunities currently exist. They confuse government bonds with savings bonds. They continue to dump money into the worst investment possible—the guaranteed investment certificate—thinking it's the right thing to do. They jump in and out of mutual funds, almost always taking a loss because they're trying to time the market. They think the holy grail in life is

Needs of retirement cause for midlife crisis

BY JADE HEMEON
BUSINESS REPORTER

maintain the comfortable lifestyle to which many middle-aged

Scott Hayman, vice-president at RBC Dominion Securities, ad-

"Anybody who hasn't started saving by their mid-40s should wake up and smell the coffee."

Source: *The Toronto Star*

paying off the mortgage, when in many cases that amounts to little more than feeding a sinkhole. And, worst of all, most people try to manage their own investments—rank amateurs in a complex financial world that demands the sharpest of minds.

If any of this applies to you, read on. Please let me show you how to change your financial life; set you on a path that will ensure financial independence; break the habits that are leading a majority of people into a worse, not a better, life.

But there is something that eclipses all other tools in importance. It's the most generous tax shelter in North America, with flexible, forgiving rules that allow assets to compound quickly. And for those who know how to apply those rules, and use them in combination, this is the tool that can build a secure future—even if you are in your forties or fifties, and have done nothing to date.

This will save you. Yes, it is the RRSP.

Do you worry about having enough money in the future? Most of us do; a recent poll showed 64% of Canadians believe they won't have enough.

I don't mean just retirement income, because, let's face it, a lot of people now in their thirties and forties may never actually retire. At least not the way my father did—leaving work in his sixties and spending the next 15 winters hitting golf balls in Florida.

Those days may be gone forever. The good pensions are harder to find now—in fact, the majority of Canadians don't have any kind of corporate pension plan.

And with the economy the way it's been so far this decade, job security—even job stability —can no longer be counted on. So, millions find themselves with multiple employers and careers, stressed out and way behind on their own retirement savings.

In fact, the country's savings rate has now dropped to 6.2% of disposable income. That is the lowest ever. It is so low, in fact, that experts like Bruce Grantier, of Scotia Investment Management, think it is impossible for it to fall further, because savings includes money that has automatically gone into pension plans and RRSP accounts. Take that away and—voluntarily—we save next to nothing.

Source:
Anthony Jenkins,
The Globe and Mail

A 1996 survey taken on the Internet by accounting firm Deloitte & Touche found that 42% of people responding to the question "How much of your income do you save?" answered: "Less than 5%." And half of those people—with solid, upper-middle-class incomes—save nothing.

Most Canadians don't have an RRSP, and, among those who do, the average saved is about $30,000. That's hardly enough to retire on. In fact, if you believe the Bank of Nova Scotia, to retire in 2020 with an income of $40,000 a year will require savings of $1.2 million. That may sound unachievable, but if you follow the strategies in this book, you can get there. I know it.

The key is to get started now, because retirement is growing much, much longer.

YEARS IN RETIREMENT

Retirement Date	Length of Retirement	
1965	8 years	(65 to 73)
1997	19 years	(65 to 84)
2010	30 years	(65 to 95)

If you retired in 1965, you needed enough savings and investment income to finance just eight years of retirement, from age 65 to 73. If you retire in 1997, you will need enough money to finance almost 20 years. And by the year 2015 (when I am 65), that could easily be closer to thirty years.

How can you amass enough money to carry yourself for three decades when you have to raise a family, pay off a mortgage and spend money on everything from insurance to university tuition? After all, the average Canadian is making the best money for only a short period of time—usually the last decade or so of his or her working life. And the Nineties downsizing is jeopardizing those good years as the older, higher-paid employees are the first to go in corporate restructuring.

> *About 350,000 Canadian men retired early—some by choice, most by job loss—in 1993. Today a third of them live in poverty. They weren't ready, because they hadn't started early enough. You must.*

Meanwhile, the government's broke, too. In his 1996 federal budget, Finance Minister Paul Martin announced the end of a key pillar of retirement—the Old Age Security (OAS) and Guaranteed Income Supplement (GIS).

In 2001, for people now under the age of sixty, they will be history, replaced with a new program called the "Seniors Benefit." Here's the catch: The new benefit will be calculated on family income, instead of on individual earnings, and it will decrease rapidly as household income rises, hitting zero at an income level that today would still see $7,000 in benefits paid each year by Ottawa.

"...IS IT JUST ME, OR DO YOU SENSE A PERVASIVE GROWING MANIA OF PENSION-RELATED PARANOIA?..........HELLO!?..."

Source: Gable, *The Globe and Mail*

So, pensions are no longer universal. In the future, only those with family incomes under $30,000 will see any substantial government income.

THE PROBLEM: OUTLIVING YOUR MONEY

Current Age	% Chance of Living Until		
(men)	**80**	**85**	**90**
30	42	24	11
40	42	25	11
50	44	26	11
60	47	28	12
65	51	30	13
70	58	34	15

Current Age	% Chance of Living Until		
(women)	**80**	**85**	**90**
30	62	45	26
40	62	45	26
50	64	46	27
60	66	48	28
65	69	50	29
70	74	54	31

Source: Statistics Canada

Let me summarize here: Most people do not have a corporate pension. Most people do not have an RRSP. Government pensions are being cut. And in about 30 years there will be twice as many retired Canadians as there are today.

Yes, this could be a recipe for disaster, but not restricted to Canada. The U.S. Labor Department says the average American spends nearly two decades in retirement now, and 20% of workers have saved absolutely nothing in any kind of investment or savings vehicle.

Part of the reason for this is real estate. Thanks to demand by Baby Boomers in the late Seventies and early Eighties, housing prices rose to artificially high levels, and the amount of mortgage debt exploded. Total mortgage debt in this country in 1985 was $116 billion, or 36% of total disposable income. By 1995, that had leapt to 65% of income, or mortgage debt of $335 billion.

And for most of that time, high housing costs helped fuel high inflation, which resulted in high mortgage-interest costs. People were so
pressed raising families and paying off substantial mortgages at high
rates that they were able to save virtually nothing for retirement.

Now, of course, a lot of those houses are starting to be paid off, and
many of them are worth less than all the money put down on them. The
average house price in Toronto in late 1989, for example, was $280,000.
By 1996 it had eroded to just $199,000—a decline of almost 30% in the
value of the single greatest asset people in that area own.

And what money most folks have been able to put together is
inevitably invested in the wrong things, usually guaranteed investment
certificates (GICs). The yield is low; the money is locked up; no capital gain is possible; and, outside of an RRSP, the tax profile is high. In
fact, as I will argue, putting money in a GIC is probably the worst
investment decision you could make.

Why do people do it?

Because the greatest risk Canadians can possibly imagine when they
think about investing is losing their money—and a GIC is "safe." In
reality, there is a greater risk.

> *The greatest risk facing us today is outliving our
> money. For most people middle-aged or younger—
> and this includes most of the Baby Boomers—it will
> happen to them. They will run out of money before
> they run out of life.*

So, it's time to change this pattern for as many people as possible,
especially you. By understanding what an RRSP is, and then harnessing the beast, you can rapidly add to your wealth. By putting your
RRSP assets into the right investments, you can have a portfolio that
takes full advantage of the outstanding conditions that will prevail as
the new millennium approaches—now just a few dozen months away.

For many people, this is the great second chance to become financially independent—maybe even wealthy, depending on how aggressive you are.

The first chance came in the Eighties, with runaway inflation and
soaring commodity prices. Those were years when your house likely
made more money than you did, and average middle-class people
could double or triple their wealth through real estate.

We know now it was largely the impact of the Baby Boomers that drove the housing market—millions of people the same age forming households and competing for real estate. Today, with that generation's housing needs met, the market has slowed and prices have dropped.

But as this generation turns 50 and starts to become obsessed with retirement needs, the next great boom will be upon us. Not in real estate this time, but in those financial products that will give the reliable double-digit annual rates of return that aging Boomers need to catch up.

This is why mutual funds will continue to escalate in value. It's why quality stocks and bonds will be in such demand. And if you know that now, in 1997—three years before the investment rush really begins—then I think you know where to invest.

And if you do it within the protective bubble of your tax-deferred RRSP, you will be making the most of this second chance.

Come with me and let's do it.

Chapter 1

Big Changes
in 1997 Rules

*They've just doubled the cost to the investor of
being fiscally prudent and responsible for their own
retirement.*

—*Kelly Rodgers, Rodgers Investment Consulting*

*Two-income Baby Boomers got slaughtered. It's a
bit of a disaster.*

—*Malcolm Hamilton, William M. Mercer Ltd.*

SENIORS BENEFIT

It came as a major surprise to the hundreds of journalists, accountants
and economists sitting with me in the federal budget lock-up in Ottawa
last March just how many changes were being made to RRSPs.

Not only was Ottawa bringing in a new Seniors Benefit, which
would gut the benefits most Baby Boomers might have received in
retirement, but here were major changes to the rules governing private
pension savings. And the budget documents were clear on why this
was happening: "The measures will limit the cost of the tax deferral
associated with retirement savings."

This was consistent with other statements made by Finance Minister
Paul Martin—that our system of RRSPs costs Ottawa billions in lost
tax revenues and he intends to get some of it back.

"They're telling above-middle-income earners that, surprise, surprise, there's nothing there for you," commented Ottawa economist
Mike McCracken.

Source: Gable, *The Globe and Mail*

The budget also pursued this theme: That taxpayers earning over $75,000 are going to be more heavily taxed. Ottawa, it said, would ensure that tax savings flowing from RRSPs would be "targeted at modest and middle-income Canadians." That has come to mean a freeze on contribution limits well into the new century.

The bottom line is clear:

- *In the future there will be less government money flowing to retired Canadians.*
- *People with above-average incomes will likely not see a single dollar from Ottawa.*
- *And wealthier Canadians now have less in the form of tax breaks to help them save for their own retirement.*

As tax expert Arthur Drache asked, incredulous, after the budget came down: "Why would a government change the rules so as to put greater impediments on private savings for retirement?"

The answer to that was in the budget documents: RRSP changes will put an extra $45 million into government coffers next year, with that figure rising to $180 million in 1998–9.

So much for a minister of Finance who said this: "In this budget, we are not raising personal taxes. We are not raising corporate taxes.

We are not raising excise taxes. In fact, we are not raising taxes."

But he was lowering tax relief. And that sure smells, feels and looks like a tax increase.

PAYING LESS TO SENIORS, STARTING IN 2001
Cut-off Income for Benefits

	Existing OAS/GIS	Seniors Benefit
Individuals	$83,500	$52,000
Families	$167,000	$78,000

Even more dramatic is the eventual replacement of the OAS and GIS programs—which were supposed to be paid to every Canadian— by the Seniors Benefit, starting in the year 2001, which will pay less to better-off Canadians, and also be calculated on the basis of family, not individual, income. That means a stunning drop in the income level at which the benefit erodes to zero.

> *Today old-age security is cut off at $83,500 in income. With the Seniors Benefit, the cut-off falls more than $30,000, to just $52,000. And for families, at a combined income of just $78,000, no cheques will arrive.*

The Seniors Benefit itself is modest, to say the least. It means that an elderly couple with no savings or other form of income—the most destitute—would receive, combined with full Canada Pension Plan payments (while the plan lasts, and who knows how long that will really be), a maximum annual allowance of about $30,000. And the amount of the Seniors Benefit falls rapidly; so, by an income level of $50,000 (including Canada Pension Plan [CPP] or Quebec Pension Plan [QPP] payments), it totals just $459 a month for a couple and just $30 a month for an individual.

For people who were 60 or older at the end of 1995, there is a choice to be made whether to sign up for the Seniors Benefit or stay on the existing OAS/GIS system.

If you're single, and your income is $36,000 or lower, you will be better off with the Seniors Benefit. But with an income above that, you're better off with the old system.

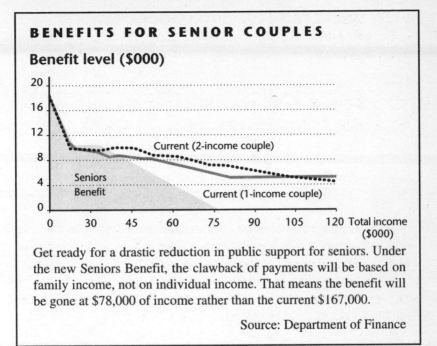

BENEFITS FOR SENIOR COUPLES

Benefit level ($000)

Current (2-income couple)

Seniors Benefit

Current (1-income couple)

Total income ($000)

Get ready for a drastic reduction in public support for seniors. Under the new Seniors Benefit, the clawback of payments will be based on family income, not on individual income. That means the benefit will be gone at $78,000 of income rather than the current $167,000.

Source: Department of Finance

The table following shows you what Ottawa expects the benefit payments will be when the system starts in 2001, by income level for singles and couples. In this case, income includes anything received from the CPP or QPP, but excludes income from the OAS or GIS, which the benefit replaces.

The saving to Ottawa in lowering the income level for benefits in 2030: $8 billion a year.

The likely combination of these changes—lowering the ability to save for retirement, gutting public pension benefits for those with higher incomes, and using family income as the basis for calculating personal wealth—is not a happy one. As pension expert Malcolm Hamilton put it in a *Globe and Mail* interview, "Between the income tax and the new seniors' benefit, you'll be turning some 60 to 70 cents on the dollar over to the government on your retirement savings. To me, this goes beyond the bounds of normal progressivity. This is almost vindictive."

According to pension consultant William Mercer Ltd., moving to the Seniors Benefit is a middle-class disaster, cutting the after-tax income of future retirees by between $3,000 and $7,000. If you are today 60 or younger, watch out!

PROJECTED LEVEL OF SENIORS BENEFIT IN 2001

Annual Seniors Benefit

Income $	Single Seniors $	Senior Couples $
0	11,420	18,440
5,000	8,920	15,940
10,000	6,420	13,440
15,000	5,160	10,940
20,000	5,160	10,320
25,000	5,160	10,320
30,000	4,350	9,510
35,000	3,350	8,510
40,000	2,350	7,510
45,000	1,350	6,510
50,000	350	5,510
60,000	—	3,510
70,000	—	1,510
80,000	—	—

The clawback of pension benefits will be relentless—with all of it taxed back at the income level of $52,000 for a single and $78,000 for a couple. And because it is now based on family income, it means seniors in the future will be doubly taxed—normal income tax on the money you receive outside of pension benefits, and then the clawback of your benefits.

> *Under the system Ottawa is proposing, if you have retirement income of more than $26,000 a year—which will be well below the poverty level—expect to lose between 42 cents and 78 cents of every dollar. In fact, many middle-class people will be actually taxed more heavily in retirement than when they were working.*

This means tax-reducing strategies will have to change for many people, especially single seniors. Boost your income during the years leading up to retirement, and then reduce taxable income for several years after age 65 in order to reduce the effect of the new clawback. Kevin Moriarty, in charge of personal retirement planning at Mercer, warns that, without careful planning, future seniors could lose up to half their savings.

And, ironically, despite all this massive change, the new system probably will fail—defeated by demographics and the coming tidal wave of retiring Baby Boomers. By the time Boomers start retiring— in 2015—the clawback will save just over 10% of the growing amount spent on seniors' pensions. But by 2015, the number of seniors will have doubled—making that reduction too insignificant to prevent a government funding crisis.

Worse, Paul Martin's rescue plan for pensions is based on the premise that wages will be 1% higher than inflation each year for the next three decades—something current conditions mock. In 1996, for example, inflation was 1.4% and the average wage gain was 1.1%. If that remains the case, pensions are cooked.

To put it mildly, we have problems. No person today more than 10 years away from retirement should count on a single dollar in public money in his or her senior years. The system might be reformed, but chances are slim. Instead, the safest assumption is that you are on your own. And, without question, the smartest thing you can possibly do is maximize your RRSP opportunities. If fact, you should be obsessed by it.

Well, here are all the new rules.

> *The message they're sending to the two-income baby boomer is, first, don't expect much, if anything, from government. Unlike your parents, no Old Age Security for you. Then they come out with another message that is: by the way, we're not going to let you help yourself, either.*
>
> —*Malcolm Hamilton, William M. Mercer Ltd.*

CONTRIBUTION LIMITS FROZEN UNTIL 2003

The 1995 budget scaled back the maximum contribution level by $1,000, to $13,500 until the end of 1997. Now that freeze has been drastically extended, which will mean people earning over $75,000 a year will be paying more tax and contributing less to their plans.

The RRSP dollar limit is now fixed for the next six years. After that it is scheduled to rise to $14,500 in 2004, and then to $15,500 in 2005—a whole decade later than that level was supposed to have been achieved.

After that, contribution limits will be indexed to the average wage, which has been barely moving higher through most of the Nineties.

This takes effect on New Year's Day, 1997, which means no plans will be registered after 1996 unless they comply with the new rules. It also means plans registered before 1997 become revocable if they don't comply with the new limits.

The impact of this seemingly small change is actually quite enormous—especially for double-income, upper-middle-class families. Most of them will simply have less to retire on in the future, because, while their ability to shelter savings is being cut, inflation is not.

So every year until the freeze is lifted (if ever), more and more taxpayers will be affected. Today the freeze affects only people making over $75,000. Within seven years it could impact on taxpayers making $65,000 in today's dollars.

DOLLAR LIMITS FOR CONTRIBUTIONS TO RRSPs

Year	Old rules	New rules
1996	$13,500	$13,500
1997	$13,500	$13,500
1998	$14,500	$13,500
1999	$15,500	$13,500
2000	Indexed	$13,500
2001		$13,500
2002		$13,500
2003		$13,500
2004		$14,500
2005		$15,500
2006		Indexed

CARRY-FORWARD LIMIT IS ELIMINATED

Since 1991, you have been allowed to carry forward for seven years RRSP contributions that you didn't, or couldn't, make for seven years.

This is a great idea, and a real blessing to people who have had a tough financial time over the last few years. If Canadians had made their maximum RRSP contributions in 1996, they would have invested a stunning $153.8 billion—which is about $130 billion more than we all actually did put in. This just shows how large the amount of unused contribution is. We are all behind in our retirement savings by that amount.

It also underscores another sobering fact: The numbers show a mere handful of Canadians are maxing out. The latest numbers show that fewer than 30% of people even make contributions and, in total, Canadians are socking away under 17% of what is allowed under the rules.

This has raised speculation that the plan is actually too rich for taxpayers unable to find the extra money each year to invest—which is one reason the maximum-contribution limit has been frozen.

But here is some good news: The seven-year limit on carrying forward those missed contributions has been eliminated. At least, for now. Ottawa says this change recognizes the fact many people go through long periods in their lives when they have no available cash—like early in careers or while raising a family—for an RRSP. The new rules allow them to catch up later in life, when they do have a larger cash flow.

> *So, while this is an improvement, it also poses a danger. If people know they can catch up later, they may be inclined to spend their money now on a better lifestyle in the knowledge no contribution room is being lost.*
> *But that would be a huge mistake.*

The real benefit comes not from how much you contribute to an RRSP, but when. Because RRSPs defer taxes until the plan is cashed in, assets within the plan are allowed to compound free of tax—so the longer an asset is in there, the greater it grows.

With RRSPs under attack, expect more changes that will further restrict your ability to catch up or to contribute significant amounts in the future. Ottawa will probably even turn around one day and eliminate this ability to carry forward unused contributions, because that only decreases revenues and increases the deficit.

According to Burlington, Ontario, chartered accountant Tim Cestnick, the writing is on the wall because Ottawa has forgotten how much money the Baby Boom generation stands to inherit over the next decade or so—money that will be socked away into RRSPs, using the carry-forward provision. That will get investors huge tax savings, and cost the government billions in lost revenues. So, political logic being what it is, the days of the carry-forward are numbered.

Cestnick is forecasting that a time limit will be reimposed on the carry-forward, and I agree—it could happen as early as the next budget, but more likely will be delayed until after the next election. But I think it will become even more serious: I believe the very ability to carry forward any unused contribution will be eliminated. Let's hope I'm wrong, and the government will not be so thick as to deny Canadians the ability to look after themselves. But just in case I might be right, there is real danger in not doing everything you can—now—to catch up completely on missed contributions. Here's how:

- Swap assets you hold outside RRSPs into the tax shelter. The rules say you don't need cash to make an RRSP contribution. Any savings bonds, GICs, mutual-fund units, strip bonds or other liquid investments will do just fine. Get them moved over now to the extent of the contributions you can carry forward.

- Borrow to invest in your RRSP. Banks, trusts, financial-services companies and others will happily lend you the money at prime. Then use the tax refund to pay down the loan. Today interest rates are cheap and the return on financial assets is high—making it a great time to use somebody else's money.

- If you do get an inheritance, dump it into an RRSP immediately.

- Lessen the taxes on your income so you can have more cash to put into an RRSP. That means less in interest income and more in dividends or capital gains. You can earn $24,000 a year in dividends before you even pay any tax. And capital gains paid by mutual funds are taxed at substantially less than income earned in interest. Besides, mutual funds are currently giving you a yield about three times higher than GICs.

- And don't wait for the next federal budget. That's retirement roulette.

- Don't make the mistake of putting off RRSP contributions to, say, pay the mortgage down. Getting rid of mortgage debt is obviously important, but if you are in your mid-forties, this could be absolutely the wrong strategy.

Meanwhile the long-term outlook for residential real estate is anything but sure. The dismal performance of real estate so far this decade may just be a taste of what is coming. With the huge Baby Boom generation aging, and a relatively small generation following, why should we think housing values will hold firm?

The average house price in Metro Toronto actually fell 31% between late 1989 and 1996. And the average house price across Canada has dropped 6% in the last year.

> *People who divert retirement savings to put it against mortgages might end up in 20 years with houses worth vastly less than the amount invested in them, and with far too little saved to live on. What a vicious lose–lose scenario.*

The new rule may be comforting now, but don't let it fool you.

ADMINISTRATION FEES ARE NOT TAX-DEDUCTIBLE

This is a typical nickel-and-dime move that will give the government a minimal amount in new revenues, but that may make some people think twice about the benefit of having a self-directed RRSP.

Now the annual administrative fee to run a self-directed plan is no longer deductible from your taxes when paid outside the plan. This fee is typically about $150 a year. As is explained in Chapter 3, in the section on self-directed RRSPs, deductible fee or not, you must have one of these.

In a post-budget interpretation, Revenue Canada says RRSP or RRIF administration fees paid outside the account will be considered a contribution to the RRSP, while fees paid inside will be considered a taxable withdrawal.

> *The message is clear—people in high income brackets are increasingly on their own when it comes to providing for their retirement.*
>
> *—Royal Trust*

INVESTMENT COUNSELLING FEES NO LONGER TAX-DEDUCTIBLE

Here was a real sleeper—contained in a single paragraph buried in a technical "Notice of Ways and Means Motion" portion of the budget. And while it does not affect many people, those it does affect will be taking a significant tax whack. As Paul Boeda, chairman of the Canadian Association of Financial Planners, said, "That came as a shock to a lot of people. It's a huge hit."

Here's why: The money wealthier people pay to have their RRSPs or RRIFs managed is clearly no longer considered a deductible expense (this had been an ambiguous area, with both tax experts and Revenue Canada officials at odds on how existing rules should be interpreted).

For example, the average client of an investment counsellor will have a minimum RRSP of $500,000—which is not that much, considering the million most of us middle-aged people will need to retire by the year 2015.

And with that much in an RRSP, it makes a lot of sense to have it professionally managed for maximum growth. But that doesn't come for free, and you can expect to pay a management fee of about 1% a year. That's $5,000—and until the 1996 budget, it was generally thought to be tax-deductible, just like the fees charged by banks and brokerages to administer a self-directed RRSP.

For someone in the top tax bracket, this clarification now means an additional $2,500 a year in tax owing—which effectively doubles the cost of having the RRSP managed.

This change will come to have a much greater significance in later years as Baby Boomers amass the capital they will need to retire with a half-decent income. If the non-deductibility of administration fees keeps people from getting the expert help they need to properly manage large RRSPs and RRIFs, then everybody—including the government—is hurt.

Somebody today in their mid-thirties, making maximum RRSP contributions for the next 30 years, will easily have a million-dollar investment to manage. And as more high-income earners today are downsized with large locked-in RRSPs that will grow over the years, they, too, will be hit with this tax that Ottawa tried so hard to hide in the back of the budget book.

AGE LIMIT DROPS FOR RRSP CONTRIBUTIONS

Here is a big change. The length of time you can contribute money into an RRSP is being cut by two years.

At a certain point in your life, the rules say you have to stop putting money away for your old age, and start taking it out—and the best way of doing that is to convert the RRSP into a RRIF (more on that later). That age had been 71, and now it's 69.

This is very significant for many reasons. Obviously it will put more money into Ottawa's coffers as two years of tax deferral are swept away. This one change means we have all potentially lost $31,000 in tax-deductible savings.

It also looks like the first step in moving the whole concept of retirement age back, from 65 to 69. Don't be surprised if that ends up being the new age at which Canada Pension Plan benefits start to flow. And it won't stop there—the age at which you must stop contributing to an RRSP and start taking money out will eventually be reduced to 65 by the time the wave of Baby Boomers reaches that point.

This likely total drop of six years in the length of time you can make contributions means billions of dollars lost in potential tax-savings for the 9 million people in my generation. It underscores the need today to take maximum advantage of the breaks that currently exist.

Source: Pritchard, *The Ottawa Citizen*

The new rule means that you will not be allowed to make an RRSP contribution or accrue pension benefits after the end of the year in which you turn 69. Then you also have to start receiving retirement income out of the plan or roll it over into a RRIF by the end of that year. Also, if you are still working, employer contributions into your plan will not be allowed.

But here's another great reason to marry somebody a lot younger than yourself: You can continue to make contributions into your spouse's plan until the year in which he or she turns 69. See the section on spousal plans in Chapter 3—one of the best ways going to split income and pay less tax. Other considerations:

- If you were 70 or older at the end of 1996, then this change does not apply to you—go ahead and operate under the old rule as if the limit were still 71.

- But if you turned 69 in 1996, then you have to move up the maturity of your RRSPs by one year, and roll them over into a RRIF by the end of 1997.

- If you had already purchased a deferred annuity before budget day (March 6, 1996), based on the old rule, then relax, you're exempt. But if you have a GIC-type RRSP with a life-insurance company, then the change will apply to you.

If you are now in your late sixties and have your RRSP locked up in five-year GICs (a bad investment choice, as I'll be arguing), then you'd better be thinking about what to do. Even if you roll the money over into a RRIF, you'll have to come up with the cash to comply with the new rule that says you have to take out a minimum amount each year, now starting at 69, instead of 71.

> *As a result of this change, it's essential for everyone to use the strategies I am presenting in this book, because you now have less money to put into an RRSP, which will be working for you for a shorter period of time.*

Hardest hit are people who are now 55 or 60 years old. Not only will many of them not be getting the public pension supplement they were counting on, but the length of time they can prepare their own retirement savings has been cut.

For them, the news is crystal clear: The great era of postwar social programs for everyone is gone.

Of course, this comes at a time when being a senior citizen is harder than ever, thanks to the low inflation and plunging interest rates that have characterized the Nineties. The average investment income for seniors has been dropping like a stone—down 10% in the latest year for which Statistics Canada has numbers.

The reason is too many seniors rely solely on interest-bearing investments like GICs for their income—an investment strategy that simply turned out to be the wrong one. I hope that as millions of Baby Boomers watch their parents struggle with a dwindling cash flow, they learn this same lesson.

The bottom line is that more and more of seniors' income is dependent on government cheques, and the government has now spelled out the fact that its cheques—starting on New Year's Day, 2001, just four dozen months from now—will be gutted.

This is indeed a wakeup call.

RETIRING ALLOWANCE ROLLOVERS PHASED OUT

This one is a killer, and it's also unfair. It should have been greeted with howls of protest when brought in by Finance Minister Paul Martin in his 1995 budget, but it slipped through, and for now we have to live with it.

The phasing-out of these rollovers will have a dramatic impact on people who lose their jobs in the future through downsizing or for other reasons. And there is every reason to expect they will number in the tens of thousands as corporations shed employees, and governments erase whole departments. If there is any one thing that has defined the Nineties so far, it is that almost everyone suffers job stress. No job seems safe anymore. And so this RRSP change could not come at a worse time.

A retirement allowance is the money you get when you retire, quit or are laid off. It's the same thing as a severance payment, and until now you have been able to roll a lot of that directly into an RRSP, and pay no tax on it.

Since the ability to roll money over into a special spousal RRSP was ended after 1994, this has been one of the few ways to get funds over your annual-contribution limit pumped into your retirement plan. (Another method is through an RRSP mortgage, which I discuss later. You may also exceed the limit in the event of a marriage breakdown, when assets are transferred, or through rollovers into a locked-in RRSP and the return of pension income plus interest into a non-locked plan.)

And a lot of middle-class people have used this effective device to minimize the tax grab on their severance packages. But starting last year (the 1996 taxation year), it is eliminated for future years.

Here is how it works:

For each year, or part of a year, prior to 1996 that you worked for your employer, you are eligible to put $2,000 into your RRSP. In addition, you can contribute $1,500 for each year prior to 1989 that you were not a part of the company's pension plan or deferred-profit-sharing plan.

> **Eligible retiring allowance**
> **(the amount of your severance package**
> **you can shelter from tax)**
> ──────────────────────────────
> **$2,000 × Years worked before 1996**
> **plus $1,500 × Years before 1989**
> **without a company pension**

For example, if you had worked for 25 years and were laid off this year, and were part of a company pension plan, you could put $46,000 into your RRSP (that's $2,000 for the 23 years worked prior to 1996).

If you worked the same length of time and never contributed to a company pension plan, the eligible RRSP contribution would be $70,000 (you add $1,500 for each of the 16 years worked prior to 1989 to the $2,000 a year for the 23 years worked prior to 1996).

Now with 1996 as the cut-off date, you will not be building up any additional rollover amount, but you will not (for now, at least) lose the amount you earned prior to last year. For people just entering the workforce, of course, it means they will never be able to take advantage of tax-free retiring allowance.

Here are some valuable tips to remember:

• Make sure you get all that's coming to you. Any part of a year—even one day—can qualify you for a full year's amount. So, if you worked from November 1993 to February 1995, the rules allow you to roll three years' worth of allowance over.

- Part-time or seasonal work also qualifies, along with co-op job placements and internships.

- Make sure you carefully review your employment record before agreeing to a settlement package. Sometimes employers are unaware that even a small part of a year worked means you can count it as a full year on the job.

- Have your employer put the money directly in an RRSP for you, and you will not have withholding tax of up to 30% deducted right off the top. You will need to fill out form TD2, called a "Tax Deduction Waiver in Respect of Funds to Be Transferred" (there's a catchy title for you). The payroll department should have that for you; if not, get it from Revenue Canada.

- If you do take the severance package itself, tax will be withheld when you are first paid. But depending how much of it you then put into an RRSP, you can get some or all of it back. Show the whole amount of the package on your income tax return at line 130, and then claim a deduction for the amount put into your retirement plan down on line 208. And attach the RRSP receipt, or the claim will be disallowed.

- If the amount you are rolling over into your RRSP is huge, you may be nailed by the alternative minimum tax, which was set up to make sure people making over $40,000 don't get enough tax deductions to reduce their income to nothing. In this case, depending on what time of year you get the money, it may be smart to take the package over a couple of tax years.

- Self-employed? Then you have also built up eligible retirement-allowance room over the years you paid yourself a salary, and can roll cash over into your RRSP. And self-employed professionals who employ their spouses can give them a one-time retirement-allowance payment when the business is being wound down.

- Finally, when you have lost your job and are offered a package, it is sometimes tempting to keep a portion in cash, instead of putting it away in the RRSP. Bad idea. You will lose up to a third of that in tax right off the top. Better to have it put in the plan with no tax deducted, and then remove what you need in small amounts (under $5,000). That way the withholding tax is only 10%.

GETTING CASH FROM YOUR RRSP

The idea is to put money into your RRSP and leave it there until you retire. But sometimes life doesn't go according to plan, and withdrawals are necessary.

You will be taxed on the money you take out, at your own marginal tax rate—which is the highest rate on the last dollar you earned. RRSP withdrawals are treated just the same as another form of income. And your bank, credit union, trust company or broker is required to withhold some of your withdrawal and send it to Ottawa.

* Because the tax rate rises with the amount withdrawn, it makes sense to take any money out in smaller amounts.

* Check on what limits your financial institution might have to discourage such small RRSP withdrawals—a limit on the number you can make, or special fees. Many don't like the paperwork withdrawals cause.

* Claim any tax withheld on your income-tax return.

TAX-WITHHOLDING RATES

	Federal	In Quebec
Up to $5,000	10%	21%
$5,000 to $15,000	20%	30%
Above $15,000	30%	35%

The changes for 1997 are indeed daunting, and the direction the latest federal budget took was truly disappointing. But do not let any of this deter you—the changes simply underscore the need to take maximum advantage of the opportunities that remain.

An RRSP is still an awesome financial vehicle. Remember this:

* Your RRSP is still the foundation of your entire investment program, and the more the benefits are reduced, the more aggressive you must become.

* As I will say often, maximize your annual contributions, and also contribute early in the tax year—not (as most people do) early in the next tax year. That can cost you tens of thousands in lost assets.

- If you have trouble finding that amount of money in a lump sum, then set up a monthly pre-authorized contribution plan. You can also use such a plan to have the taxes withheld on your payroll reduced. I will show you how to do that in Chapter 5, on RRSP strategies.

- Or borrow to get the money. Most banks, trusts, credit unions and many brokers or planners will lend you the money at prime, or cheaper. Use the tax refund to pay the loan down, and you will be ahead of the game.

- Finally, by all means, take action now. Another federal budget is coming and it could contain just as many significant changes stripping you of more ability to save. Don't be frozen in the headlights. It could be a big, big truck coming.

Chapter 2

The Greying of Canada

"**G**overnments have a mind-boggling unfunded pension liability. In the U.S., this liability—the sum that would have to be set aside today to cover the value of future benefits minus trust-fund balances and all future Social Security taxes at current values—amounts to 43% of the value of the economy's annual output.

> *In Germany, it is 160%. In Japan, 200%. In Canada, 250%."*
> —*Organization for Economic Co-operation and Development*

> *If the existing schedule of contribution rates is not increased and benefits continue as now legislated, the CPP fund is expected to be exhausted by the year 2015.*
> —*Bernard Dussault, Chief Actuary, Office of the Superintendent of Financial Institutions Canada*

Unbelievable changes are in store for Canadian society over the next three decades. Almost 10 million people will be retired.

The fastest-growing age category over the next four years will be 45 to 54 years old—by the turn of the century, in Canada alone, there will be 400,000 more of these middle-aged people. And the fastest-growing age group over the next 20 years will be that of people over 80.

The cost of health care will rise by 50%. The value of most residential real estate will likely plunge. Governments, still carrying debts that took decades to build up, will not be able to provide medical and pension benefits to the retired without drastically increasing taxes on those working.

Source: Gable, *The Globe and Mail*

But tax increases of that size are simply not possible. Already Canadians pay punishingly high taxes compared with Americans. And why should aging Baby Boomers, who today are saving just a fraction of what they will need in retirement, cast this burden off on Generation Xers?

In the United States, where the situation is much less desperate, the tax increase necessary to support today's middle-aged in retirement "would be very close to absorbing all the lifetime income for future workers," according to University of California economist Alan Auerbach.

The Canadian Institute of Actuaries made it clear in a landmark 1994 report on the future—which was virtually ignored by the federal government—"We are asking a generation of Canadians to forgo increases in their standard of living for the best part of their working lifetime.

"If real wages do not increase, we are asking them to accept a significant reduction in their standard of living."

And we are asking too much.

That was acknowledged in a chilling 1996 report by the C.D. Howe Institute, which stated the obvious: Today's relatively well-off middle-aged and middle-class taxpayers will have to shoulder more burden.

"Fiscal retrenchment should be focused so that more of the costs fall on well-to-do Canadians," the report *Beyond the Deficit: Generation X and Sustainable Debt* concluded.

To do that, urged McMaster University economist William Scarth, government must, among other things:

- Toughen up pension rules for the wealthy,

- Impose user fees, and

- End the universality of social programs.

To a large extent, that is clearly the direction the federal government is heading in. When the new Seniors Benefit clicks in on January 1, 2001, replacing the current OAS and GIS, universality of social programs will be officially dead.

But taxing the wealthy alone is not enough. Scarth also argues that the future will be bleak unless Ottawa balances its budget within three years, and then runs a surplus for the next decade, vastly reducing the level of federal debt.

All indications are, however, that is just not going to happen. As I write this, Finance Minister Paul Martin has set no target for reducing the annual operating deficit to zero. And until that point is reached, the country's debt will continue to grow—along with the inevitable problems down the road.

This is why it is so critical that we all maximize RRSPs now—sheltering income from an increasing tax load, harnessing the power of rising financial markets and building a defence against what could be a desperate time beyond the year 2015.

And things stand to be a lot more difficult in Canada than elsewhere around the world. Proportionate to the size of the population, Canada had the biggest Baby Boom generation in the world. That means it will also likely have the biggest retirement crisis.

The country's birth rate—like that in Japan and Europe—is now below the replacement level. If immigration to Canada were to stop, the country would gradually empty until nobody lived here.

And because of our relatively small population, Canada is overly dependent for its prosperity on trade. But our main trading partners also have aging populations, and face similar domestic problems—a threat to sustained trade and productivity in the years to come.

In 1990 less than 20% of the population in OECD countries was over 60. But the World Bank says that, by 2030, that will have risen by half, to more than 30%.

A huge part of this problem is caring for the health of a rapidly aging population. Up to 90% of a person's total lifetime medical costs can be incurred in the last six months of life.

That certainly was driven home to me as I watched my father

succumb to Alzheimer's disease in late 1995, living first in a full-care nursing home costing $6,000 a month, then in hospital with around-the-clock attention. He was institutionalized for almost two years, about average for today's 84-year-olds.

> *The Baby Boom and subsequent baby bust have clearly created a tidal wave of shifting demo-graphics. The transition from a young population to an old one will have profound consequences for our society . . .*
>
> —*Canadian Institute of Actuaries*

"Demographic changes over the next 25 years mean that we will have to restrain our appetites for health care services just to maintain today's level of spending relative to economic growth," said a 1996 report on health care by the Canadian Institute of Actuaries.

"But the situation is not that simple. The demographic shift to an aging population means the inherent demand for heath care services will actually increase significantly. At the same time, there is a growing consensus that today's level of spending on health care is already excessive."

The actuaries were painfully clear: Future costs of the current medical system are "unaffordable." Caring for today's population will cost today's taxpayers $1 trillion—something most people are completely unaware of yet.

"In the short run, until about the year 2000, the earning power of the Baby Boomers will go a long way towards supporting existing spending patterns," the report said.

"However, just after the turn of the century, the situation will change significantly. The leading edge of the age bulge reaches 55 in the year 2000, and begins to retire. That will have the two-edged effect that the productive base will begin to shrink and the high health care–user group will expand."

That's when it hits the fan. If nothing is done, each worker in 2031 will have to produce 60% more than he or she did in 1991 to care for senior dependants.

And that is impossible.

So, the report called for an actual rationing of health care, along with a new emphasis on preventative medicine and a major cost control by government.

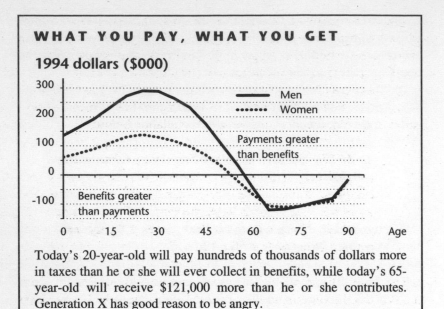

WHAT YOU PAY, WHAT YOU GET

1994 dollars ($000)

Today's 20-year-old will pay hundreds of thousands of dollars more in taxes than he or she will ever collect in benefits, while today's 65-year-old will receive $121,000 more than he or she contributes. Generation X has good reason to be angry.

Source: Institute for Research on Public Policy

Will this happen?

It's doubtful. Our Baby Boomer–dominated society and political structure is still funding health care on the pay-as-you-go basis—just like the endangered Canada Pension Plan.

That means today's Boomers are paying for the health care being consumed by their aged parents. Tomorrow it will be Generation X faced with a stunning health bill to fund the hip replacements and prostate-gland removals of legions of retired Baby Boomers.

Today the estimated health-care bill for people over 65 for the rest of their lives is $369 billion. But the health bill for all the people who are working today, over the course of their lives, is $1 trillion—most of it payable in about 30 years.

But payable by whom?

> *We all know by now that the current structure of Canada's fiscal policy is unsustainable from an economic standpoint. It is also immoral. We simply cannot continue borrowing against the future of our children.*
>
> —Monique Jerome-Forget, Institute for Research on Public Policy

Take a close look at the following graph showing the age structure of the country. Today it looks close to what the "proper" age structure of any society should be—a pyramid, with more younger people at the bottom, tapering to narrow bands of older citizens at the top.

But this pyramid is about to disappear, turning into a mushroom—incredibly—with thicker bands of old people in their sixties and seventies at the top, dwarfing the younger population below.

> *By 2031—thirty-four years from now, when today's youngest Baby Boomers contemplate retirement— the largest single population group will be women aged 65. The second-largest group will be women aged 70. There will be, in fact, more 75-year-old women than girls under 10.*

The implications of this are mind-boggling. Dealing with them should be at the very top of the national political agenda. The fact that it is not pretty well guarantees the future is going to be a dark place for the unprepared.

Retirement financing for today's Baby Boomers will be tough enough. For people in their twenties and thirties, it will be a nightmare unless drastic change occurs.

In its 1996 report, the Institute for Research on Public Policy proved that people in this age category will each pay hundreds of thousands more in taxes than they will receive in benefits—because of the cost of health care and other benefits for the previous, aging generation.

For these people, the future holds little other than substantial tax increases, which will make retirement planning and saving that much more difficult. It is an utter condemnation of the generations now working or in retirement that this should have come to pass. And it is our responsibility to try to change things before it is too late.

But according to the IRPP, correcting the intergenerational imbalance would mean gutting today's benefits for seniors; raising taxes each year, permanently, by 1.2%; and cutting government purchases a massive 10.4%.

Without that kind of action, this is how the tax and benefit scorecard looks:

Age and sex now	Get more in benefits	Pay more in taxes
Newborn boy		$131,200
Newborn girl		$56,700
25-year-old man		$290,000
25-year-old woman		$136,000
65-year-old man	$121,400	
65-year-old woman	$108,100	

Canada's population profile makes this about the worst country in the world to have the kind of social programs that we do—namely, pay-as-you-go. The tidal wave of aging Boomers will drive that home in a dramatic, destructive way.

A person born in 1911, for example, will get a 22.4% return on the money he paid out in Canada Pension Plan contributions. A person born today will get a rate of return of about 1.5% on all the money he or she will pay in during a whole lifetime. As the actuaries point out in a 1996 report on the future of the public pension plan, it was "enacted in 1965, when Canada was nearing the end of an unprecedented 20-year economic boom. The economy had grown quickly in real terms. Interest rates, nominal and real, were low.

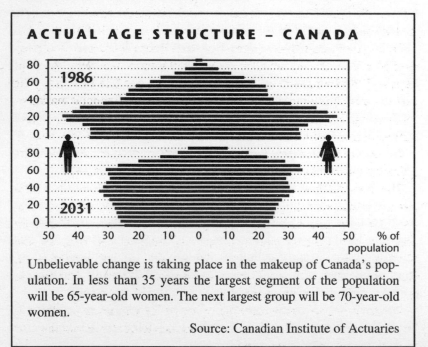

ACTUAL AGE STRUCTURE – CANADA

Unbelievable change is taking place in the makeup of Canada's population. In less than 35 years the largest segment of the population will be 65-year-old women. The next largest group will be 70-year-old women.

Source: Canadian Institute of Actuaries

Source: *The Financial Post*

"Economists believed that this environment, and the concurrent baby boom, would endure and that pay-as-you-go systems could ride a wave of prosperity."

Ironically, the great Baby Boom ended about 18 months after the Canada Pension Plan was created—with its whole funding premise that the babies would never stop coming.

Today, incredibly, Ontario teachers have more money in their pension plan than the whole CPP does. The Ontario Teachers' Pension Plan in 1996 had assets of $41.9 billion, up from $25 billion a year earlier—reflecting the plan's investments in rising financial markets.

The Canada Pension Plan's reserve fund at the same time was at $41 billion, and shrinking fast as payroll deductions fell behind payouts.

Given the population makeup, the CPP is cooked. Any serious retirement planning should include no public pension income.

The slow death of the pay-as-you-go pension plan proves that. The old are outpacing the young. The takers will outnumber the contributors. The long-term outlook for both public pensions and the Canadian economy is not a rosy one. Yes, financial markets will rise, and the North American economy improve, for at least a decade, maybe more. But beyond that, things will get a lot tougher. Especially for people my age—who are not prepared for what we know is coming.

We are powerless to reverse the aging of the Canadian population. So we must do more to prepare for it, and then to continue building our financial assets while in retirement.

I urge you to follow the strategies in this book to do just that. Today's RRSP rules, although more restrictive than in 1996, are still fluid and flexible enough to provide you with a comfortable income, if you take action now, and continue year in and year out for the rest of your life.

> *The bad news is that, based on the evidence, taxes will go up in the future, not down. The level of government support will fall. Most of today's middle-aged people will receive no public pensions. It's entirely possible that all of today's younger taxpayers will get nothing.*

There will be a health-care crisis so long as the country tries to keep a universal, public, free-access system. Faced with millions more elderly people, either care will have to be rationed—forcing patients south of the border for treatments—or the system will have to be at least partially privatized. Either way, it's going to cost a lot more to get sick in 2020 than it does today.

In this context, financial fitness should go hand in hand with physical fitness. RRSPs and preventative health practices are your two best friends.

But there is good news, too.

RRSP investors today face wonderful, almost unparalleled, opportunities to make their money grow. The aging population means lower inflation, and that will also knock down interest rates over the long term.

The value of real assets—real estate, gold, Porsches—will decline, and the value of financial assets will rise. Quality stocks, bonds and mutual funds will catapult higher in value as money flows out of those real assets.

At the same time the Baby Boom generation is entering its peak earning and spending years. A growing number of people in this age group have the mortgage paid off, giving them more disposable income. And just as millions of people hit age 50 at the same time, starting in the year 2000, they will do to stocks, bonds and funds what they did to real estate in the Eighties—driving valuations higher as they all scramble to invest in the same places.

If you know that now, in 1997, then I think you know where to invest. And you know where not to invest.

> *This is a time for the middle-aged and older to be systematically removing equity from residential real estate and transferring it to financial assets.*

Yes, for many people, this is a shocking notion, because it means borrowing against your paid-up house and getting the money into assets like equities and mutual funds. This does not mean selling your home—although for many that is a good option—but rather diversifying through a home-equity loan. Canadians have 70% of their net worth in residential real estate, which is far too much, and which leaves them far less diversified than they should be. Besides, residential real estate faces a bleak long-term future.

For millions of house-rich and RRSP-poor Boomers, this is the only course to follow. Your house has probably gone down in value (unless you live in Vancouver—and there, well, just wait) and there are more reductions to come. Meanwhile, equity-based mutual funds that track stock-market performance have been growing by double digits.

With low inflation and low interest rates, at a time when there are strong corporate profits, those booming financial markets will continue to boom. For people serious about growing their wealth, the timing could hardly be better.

And there is no easier way to accomplish this magic than within an RRSP. Here's how . . .

AN EXTRA WEIGHT ON THEIR SHOULDERS

	1994		2036	
Population	29,248,100	100%	38,800,000	100%
15–64	19,811,000	68%	23,700,000	61%
65+	3,472,500	12%	8,700,000	22%

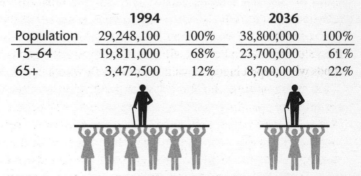

Canadian workers are going to face a retiree crisis. In 1994, there were six workers to support each senior. In less than forty years, there will be a senior to support for every three workers. Either taxes will have to rocket higher or retirement support payments plunge. Will the people being born today put up with more taxes than you pay?

Source: Statistics Canada

Chapter 3

Life in the Bubble

Government-backed pensions have proven both unsustainable and very difficult to reform. Many are nearing collapse.

—*The World Bank*

No procrastination is possible, especially for the Baby Boomers, who are still paying off their debts.

—*Jean-Paul Choucha, Royal Trust Wealth Management*

It hit me one day when a very successful, globe-trotting woman I work with at CFTO Television in Toronto came up and asked me, "Garth, should I cash in my mutual funds this year to buy an RRSP?"

She had absolutely no idea what an RRSP is. I was amazed, then I realized there was no reason she should know, because schools don't teach it and all the companies selling RRSPs don't bother explaining what it is and how it works.

So, I told her to think about her mutual funds, which were growing in value and all exposed to capital-gains tax. "Now," I said, "imagine if you put those funds inside a protective bubble which shielded them from tax. The bubble is called an RRSP."

So, she did. With one phone call she opened a self-directed RRSP and transferred the mutual funds—$15,000 worth—into the plan. And for making the call, she got an RRSP rebate—a cheque from the government for $8,100. Now she had tax-free investments and 54% more money than before she picked up the phone. And I had a new friend.

An RRSP is not a product that you buy at the bank. But thousands— maybe millions—of Canadians believe just that. So, they happily dump billions of dollars into low-yield savings instruments like GICs never even knowing there is a world of sexy alternatives.

An RRSP is not a thing; instead, it's a process. It was a way for my friend at CFTO to shelter her investments from tax. It was a way for her to save $8,000 on her income taxes. And, of course, it's the best possible way to save for retirement.

RRSPs were created in 1957, even before we had a public pension plan, and were always intended to be the principal pillar of retirement planning. But it's only been in the past decade that people have come to realize just how valuable and powerful they can be.

Most members of my own Baby Boom generation are at risk, and afraid. Job insecurity, government downsizing, corporate restructuring—these are realities of the Nineties that are now nightmares for those middle-aged Canadians who have no retirement savings. We are now behind by $158 billion—the amount we all could have put into RRSPs, and have not. In the entire generation, only 5 million of us have started saving, using this wonderful tool.

The rest are paying more taxes than they have to. Their investments are underperforming. They are victims of inflation, and most of them are in deep denial.

Let's run through the basic rules. Here is all you really need to know.

RRSPs: THE BASICS AT A GLANCE

What is an RRSP?

A good question most Canadians can't answer. An RRSP is a registered retirement savings plan that lets you defer taxes on money saved today. The idea is to encourage you to save by letting you put off paying those taxes until you retire—when most of us are in a lower tax bracket, and will pay less tax on those savings.

The benefits of opening an RRSP and contributing to it every month or year are enormous. First, all the money put in the plan is deducted from your taxable income, meaning most people get big tax-refund cheques. You can then use that extra money to invest.

Second, your taxable investments (GICs, mutual funds, stocks, bonds) can be put in your RRSP, and suddenly will grow in value tax-free. I don't care what anybody tells you about investments, but there is no faster way to build wealth than doing it within an RRSP. None.

Third, when you retire, you can roll your RRSP assets over into a

RRIF (registered retirement income fund), which further defers taxes and lets them grow tax-free, so long as you agree to take a minimal amount out of the plan every year.

And, fourth, you can save a bundle on lifetime taxes because, by deferring taxation until later in life—and using an RRSP to split income between you and your less-taxed spouse—in most cases you will be taxed at a lower marginal rate.

Simply put: This is the best leg-up on the future you're going to get. In fact, the RRSP rules are so generous, flexible and accommodating it's hard to believe they exist in this country, where we are taxed to death compared with our American neighbours.

Who can have an RRSP?

Anybody who earns income can have an RRSP until the end of the year in which you turn 69. Then you should convert it into a RRIF and start taking money out. You can also continue putting money into your spouse's RRSP, no matter what your age, until that spouse turns 69.

There is no minimum age—so long as you earn income.

How much can I put in?

That depends on how much income you make. If you work for a company that has a pension plan, your maximum contribution for the 1996 tax year is 18% of your 1995 income, minus a pension adjustment, to a maximum of $13,500.

For those without a company plan, the top contribution is 18% of income, once again to a maximum of $13,500. To reach that contribution level, your income has to be $75,000, which puts you in the top 6% of Canadians.

As noted already, the 1996 federal budget slammed the door on plans to move the contribution level higher. It is now frozen until the year 2004.

What if I miss a contribution?

Relax—you can catch up later on missed contributions. But you can never catch up on the tax-free income those contributions could have earned during all the time you did not play.

The latest budget removed a restriction limiting the ability to carry forward missed contributions for only seven years. Now it is unlimited, but never use that as an excuse not to chip in all you can.

What if I contribute too much?

You are allowed to make an overcontribution, without penalty, so long as it doesn't exceed $2,000 during your lifetime. That limit used to be $8,000, but was drastically scaled back in the 1995 budget. It might disappear completely in the 1997 one—so take advantage now.

You don't get a tax deduction for an overcontribution, but it can still grow tax-free within your plan. And you can use it in future years for future RRSP payments.

Overcontributions can be withdrawn, but in most cases you will be charged withholding tax—which you claim back on your income-tax return by filing Form 3012A.

If your overcontribution exceeds the $2,000 limit, Revenue Canada will box your ears, charging you a penalty of 1% a month on the extra until it is removed. And be aware that children under 18 at the beginning of the year can't make the overcontribution.

When can I make a contribution?

Anytime. Earlier is better. And doing it monthly is great.

A lot of people think they can only make a contribution in January or February—that "RRSP season" of the year.

But that is not the case. RRSP season has evolved because most people leave doing important things until the last minute, and the deadline for making a contribution that will earn you a tax break is within 60 days of the end of the year. That means the deadline for saving on 1996 taxes is March 1, 1997.

Of course, don't miss that deadline. But you should also be contributing as early in the year as possible—for that tax year, not the previous one. This means your money compounds for an extra whole year, and just by changing the day on which you make your contribution, not the amount, you can be tens of thousands of dollars ahead in retirement.

Or, because it's hard to find a big pile of extra money each year, you can contribute monthly. A regular RRSP payment soon becomes like a car loan—something you forget about. An increasing number of smart people are saving this way.

What kind of tax break do I get?

A big one. And, unlike most of the rest of life, the more money you make, the bigger the break.

The entire amount of the contribution you make is deducted from your taxable income. So if you contribute $5,000 and you are in the 40% tax bracket, you save $2,000. If you are in the 54% tax bracket, you save $2,700.

Of course, this could change in the future. The tax credit system could be applied, which would reduce the tax break for upper-income earners. That, in turn, increases the wisdom of making maximum contributions now.

What can go in my RRSP bubble?

A huge number of financial assets can go into an RRSP, but most people—wrongly—put their retirement savings in GICs or savings bonds. These offer no risk, but they also give very low rates of return. Investors who don't want any risk could get a far higher rate of return with government strip bonds. More on that in Chapter 5, on RRSP strategies. Other things you can put in your RRSP include:

- mutual funds

- term deposits

- Canadian stocks

- corporate strip bonds

- federal and provincial government bonds

- Crown corporation bonds

- foreign government bonds

- limited-partnership units

- labour-sponsored venture-capital funds

- small-business shares

- mortgages

- your own mortgage

What can't be in my RRSP?

Real estate, precious metals, foreign currency, art, antiques, put options, commodities or futures. That pretty well covers it.

But existing rules allow you to put real-estate or gold mutual funds or stocks in your RRSP. You can have bonds or other securities denominated in foreign currencies in there as well.

How many RRSPs can I have?

Just as many as you want. You can have several RRSPs at several financial institutions—but I wouldn't recommend it. Each plan—if it's self-directed (and it should be)—costs about $150 a year to administer, and that money is no longer tax-deductible. In addition, there are often transaction fees. And human nature being what it is, it's sometimes hard to manage multiple plans.

So my choice has been to have just one, big, self-directed plan managed by a smart financial adviser. It can invest in a number of things—equity mutual funds, stocks, federal and provincial government bonds, Crown corporation bonds and corporate bonds (that's what's in my RRSP).

With one plan, my costs are kept in check, and it's easy to measure the monthly performance of the investments in it.

Can I deduct interest on an RRSP loan?

Sorry, no. That used to be the case, but no longer. Now loans taken out to make an RRSP contribution are not tax-deductible.

But that doesn't mean you should not borrow. Indeed, borrow all you need to make the annual maximum allowable contribution. Here's why:

• Most banks and trusts and credit unions will give you an RRSP loan at their best rate—usually prime. Many brokerages or financial-planning companies will even give you money at well below the prime rate, so long, of course, as they are managing your portfolio. In any case, with today's low rates, this is cheap, cheap money.

• Making an RRSP contribution in most cases will net you a fat tax refund. Just take that cheque along to where you borrowed the money and use it to pay down a major part of that loan.

• With any kind of astute investing, say in conservatively managed, equity-based mutual funds, you will earn tax-free returns well in excess of the cost of borrowing.

• As a general rule of thumb, if you can pay off the RRSP loan within a year—by the time you need to take out another one—you're doing just fine.

Here is an example of why it's smart to borrow so you can make the maximum annual RRSP contribution. Let's say you have $5,000 to invest, but under the rules you could put in $10,000. How much ahead would you be by borrowing the other $5,000?

	Invest $5,000	Invest $10,000 (with a loan)
Tax refund at 40% rate	$2,000	$4,000
Invest in a government bond yielding 7%	350	700
You're ahead by this much	$2,350	$4,700
Use refund to pay down loan		-4,000
Repay rest of loan at 7%		-1,070
Net gain	$2,000	-1,070
RRSP assets	$5,350	$10,700
Total assets	$7,350	$9,630

How about foreign content?

Yes, you want foreign content in your RRSP, because we still have this little problem in Canada called Lucien Bouchard. If (or when) there is another referendum in Quebec, short-term interest rates will jump, and the dollar will tumble—just like every other time there's been a national-unity crisis. In addition, the dollar has weakened steadily for years against currencies like the German mark and Japanese yen.

So it is a smart thing not to have all your eggs in one basket or all your wealth in Canadian dollars.

The rules allow you to have up to 20% of the total book value of your RRSP in foreign securities. There is considerable pressure being put on Ottawa to raise that to 30%, and eventually let you invest in whatever the heck you want to, regardless of what currency it is denominated in. I believe the rules will be changed, for the better, but until they are, make sure you stick as close to that 20% as you can.

For most people, the common foreign investments are U.S. equity or global mutual funds. There's more on that below, in the section on foreign content.

Can I use my RRSP to buy a house?

You sure can, under the Home Buyers' Plan. First-time buyers can withdraw up to $20,000 for a down-payment or, with your spouse, up to $40,000. The money has to be paid back into the plan, but you get 15 years to do that.

Simply put, this is the only way I know of getting $40,000 free of tax and without interest.

The Home Buyers' Plan exists largely thanks to the lobbying efforts of the Canadian Real Estate Association, home builders and other housing groups. I remember, as a member of Parliament in the early Nineties, how hard and effectively they pushed to get this change. And since it started, the plan has been wildly successful in helping first-timers, especially when combined with the 5% down now allowed by the Canada Mortgage and Housing Corporation.

But there is controversy. Some people think that by letting you take money out of your RRSP to buy a home, you are corrupting the whole retirement-savings system. After all, it was set up to finance retirement, not to help people buy houses.

There is some logic in that, although the Home Buyers' Plan has done much to help improve the economy so far this decade. The most important thing to remember is that money removed from your RRSP is no longer compounding tax-free. Instead, it has been put into an investment (real estate) that does not have a good long-term future—at least, most residential real estate (there are exceptions—namely, housing that will be in demand as the population ages).

If it were me, I'd leave my money in the RRSP.

What about my severance package?

The best possible place to stash the money you might get on being laid off or fired (or even just retired) is your RRSP. The rules allow termination payments (technically called "retiring allowances") to be rolled over right into an RRSP. If it is done directly by your former employer, then no tax is withheld. If you get a cheque and then put the money in an RRSP, you will lose 30% of it in taxes—which you can claim back later on your tax return.

You're allowed to put in $2,000 for each year you worked before 1996. In addition, you can also put in $1,500 for each year you worked and did not contribute to a company pension plan before 1989.

Can I split income with an RRSP?

Absolutely. And you should. You do not want to end up in retirement with the bulk of your family assets in the name of the person who pays the most tax—but that is exactly what happens with most Canadians.

Typically, the husband makes the most money, makes the most investments and ends up in the top marginal tax bracket, because the couple's income is flowing in through his fingers. That family could vastly improve its income level and standard of living by simply shifting assets into the name of the lower-taxed spouse. And there is no easier or more effective way of doing that than a spousal RRSP.

You're allowed to contribute to your husband's or wife's RRSP, up to the same level you could put money into your own plan. After a short period of time, those assets then belong to the other person and, when cashed in, are taxed at his or her rate, not yours.

Makes a lot of sense. Do it.

Can I transfer between RRSPs?

Yes, Revenue Canada imposes no penalties for transfers, but switches can often be a real hassle. Why? Because financial institutions do not like to send money to other institutions, and they are cranky about it. I have even run into instances where so little attention was given to money flowing out of a bank that it was completely lost!

Expect to pay a fee to the bank or trust when you move RRSP money, and expect delays. Make sure the paperwork is in to the bank long before the switch is to take place, then hope for the best.

> *TIP: The company to which you are transferring your RRSP will be happy for the business—probably happy enough to pay the fee from the transferring company.*

What happens when I die?

Hey, this is Canada—you pay tax. Upon death, an RRSP is deemed to be cashed out, which means your estate pays big bucks in tax because the whole amount is added to your taxable income that year.

This is why you should not write "Estate" on that part of the RRSP application that asks you who should be the beneficiary. Unfortunately, not enough people realize this and their survivors see a big inheritance disappear in taxes.

You can roll your entire RRSP assets over, free of tax, to your spouse simply by naming him or her as the beneficiary.

Or you can give any infirm children or grandchildren under 18 who are dependent upon you the same tax-free gift, without having to pay probate fees. Or you can designate your RRSP to buy an annuity to look after a healthy dependent child or grandchild until he or she becomes 18.

Now, what happens if you do not have a spouse or offspring, and designate somebody else as beneficiary?

Most important, there is no way to transfer those assets to somebody without tax implications. So your bank or trust company will treat that as a simple withdrawal of the RRSP and send your estate a T4RSP tax slip. Then your estate has to pay what is probably going to be a very large tax bill.

This becomes tricky.

If you have $100,000 in an RRSP and another $100,000 in assets when you die, and you want to leave the money equally to two friends or relatives, you have to do it carefully. If you name one as the beneficiary of your RRSP, then a tax bill of about $50,000 will be payable—not by the beneficiary, but by the estate.

That means the beneficiary will get the full $100,000, but the second person, named as the inheritor of your estate, will get only $50,000, after the tax bill is paid.

So, in this case, it would be fairer to name the estate as the beneficiary of the RRSP, and the two friends or relatives as the joint inheritors. That way, at least, the tax owing would be shared equally by both (but probate would be liable).

Some other things to consider:

- If you die without designating your spouse as the beneficiary of your RRSP, but if he or she is the beneficiary of your estate (as spelled out in your will), then it's still okay. Your spouse can get the money by filling our Form T2019, and the RRSP assets will be transferred, tax free.

- Children stop being children, as Revenue Canada sees it, when they turn 18. That means that beyond that age you cannot roll your RRSP assets over to them without being taxed. (The exception is an infirm child or grandchild, regardless of age.) That means you must review your will and RRSP documents on a regular basis.

- Ditto with the marriage. The divorce rate is astonishingly high in this country and, by law, retirement assets are divided equally upon divorce, because—like the house, cottage, car and furniture—they are considered "family assets" under most provincial laws. Marriage breakdown is unique in that it is the only situation in which both RRSPs and pension assets are divided equally between husband and wife.

That can lead to a situation in which, in order to keep his own company pension, a man may have to sign over RRSP assets in his name to his spouse. Or what's in an RRSP in a wife's name could be swapped for the family real estate, if they were of nearly equal value. Sound messy? It sure can be.

And if a marriage collapse is on the horizon, the spouse who's been making contributions might want to stop—saving his or her contribution "room" for future years, when the separation is history and the RRSP sharing is over.

But all that doesn't mean your former spouse has to get the other half if you die first. Make sure you change the beneficiary designation at the bank or trust or brokerage where your RRSP lives. Divorce will automatically change the designation in your will, but not at the institution. And if you remarry, ensure your new spouse is the new beneficiary.

That will help get things off on the right foot.

HOW MUCH CAN YOU CONTRIBUTE?

As I pointed out in the previous pages, the feds have once again messed around with RRSP contribution levels. The 1996 budget came in with some major changes, one being freezing the maximum at $13,500 well into the next century.

This was done for political reasons, addressing the perception some people have that "rich" Canadians are taking too much advantage of the RRSP system. In general, the freeze affects only those people earning over $75,000. Combined with the two-year drop in the time allowed to contribute, this change will have major negative implications for tens of thousands of middle-class Canadians in the decades to come.

You are allowed to contribute a certain percentage of your earned income (note: that's money you earned by working or having rental income, not money your investments earned) every year into an RRSP, to the allowable maximum. Only a tiny number of Canadians actually put in the maximum each year, because they either don't earn enough or, if they do, don't have that much extra cash.

One of the very best RRSP strategies possible is to contribute to your plan early in the tax year. That means you should make your 1997 contribution on Thursday, January 2, 1997. But how do you know how much you are allowed in that year? You will not receive your annual T4 slip from your employer until February, to see what your pension adjustment is. You may not really know how much money you will make in 1997. And Revenue Canada will not be sending you a statement of how much you can put into the RRSP, based on 1996 income, until sometime in the summer.

The simple way is to guess—after all, you can fine-tune your plan later in the year, when Revenue Canada does notify you.

Or you can call Revenue's TIPS line—it is listed in the blue pages of your phone book under Revenue Canada, Taxation (Can 48 section). Have last year's tax return handy, along with your social insurance number. The computer will talk to you for a while and then tell you your limit, including missed past contributions

But if you are one of those hands-on people who wants the accurate and complicated approach, well, here we go.

If you don't have a company pension plan
Then it's all quite simple. In 1997, you can contribute 18% of the money you earned in 1996, to a maximum of $13,500. Plus you can catch up on past contributions, plus you can overcontribute once, to the limit of $2,000.

If you do have a company pension plan
It's the same procedure, but you need to take into account your pension adjustment, which can be found in Box 52 of the T4 slip you get in February.

You can contribute 18% of your earned income to a maximum of $13,500, less the amount of the pension adjustment.

How to determine your "earned income"
This is the tricky part, because some of your income is allowed when calculating RRSP contribution limits, and some is not.

Here is what qualifies as "earned income":

- Employment earnings

- Self-employment earnings

- Rental income (after expenses, like mortgage payments)

- Royalties and advances (authors and inventors)

- Research grants

- CPP and QPP disability payments

- Taxable long-term disability payments
- Employee profit-sharing-plan allocations
- Supplementary employment-insurance benefits
- Alimony and child support
- Director's fees
- Any taxable benefits showing up on your T4 slip

And here is a partial list of income that does not qualify you to increase your RRSP contribution limit:

- Employment-insurance benefits
- CPP or QPP retirement benefits
- Investment interest (GICs, etc.)
- Capital gains
- Dividend income
- Pension income
- Business income for limited partners
- Scholarships or bursaries

Now, once you have added together all your earned income, reduce that amount by subtracting a few things, including:

- Union dues
- Alimony payments
- Self-employment losses
- Professional dues
- Deductible employment expenses
- Rental losses

And there you have it: your "earned income." Multiply it by 18%, then deduct your pension adjustment from that amount and that is your allowed 1997 RRSP contribution, so long as it does not exceed $13,500. Add to it any unused contribution "room" from the past, and subtract any overcontributions beyond the new $2,000 limit.

Contribution calculator to determine your 1997 RRSP contribution limit

1. *Determine your 1996 "earned income" using the worksheet that follows.*
2. *Multiply that "earned income" by 18%. That amount or $13,500—whichever is less—is your contribution base.*
3. *Find out what your pension adjustment will be. It's on the T4 slip your employer will send by the end of February 1997. If you want to make an earlier contribution, call your company's payroll department to get the pension adjustment, or a good idea of what it will be.*
4. *Subtract that pension adjustment from your RRSP contibution base. That's how much money you can put into your plan in 1997.*

WORKSHEET FOR CALCULATING EARNED INCOME

Add together:	Line on 1996 tax return	Amount
Total employment earnings (T4 slips)	101–104	_____
Net rental income	104	_____
Alimony or child-care income	128	_____
Self-employment income	135–143	_____
Taxable disability payments	114,152	_____
Employee profit-sharing allocation	104	_____
Research grants	104	_____
Supplementary employment-insurance benefits	104	_____
Author or inventor royalties	104	_____
Taxable benefits (from T4)		_____
Total		_____
Subtract from that:		
Union or professional dues	212	_____
Alimony or support payments	220	_____
Rental losses	126	_____
Self-employment losses	135–143	_____
Tax-deductible expenses	229	_____
Total		_____
1996 earned income		_____

If you are not a member of a company pension plan, then it is simpler. You just take 18% of your total earned income and contribute whatever is less—that amount, or $13,500.

And if you earned more than $75,000 in 1996, you don't need to do the 18% calculation. Just take $13,500 as your limit if you do not have a company pension, or $13,500 less the pension adjustment, if you do.

BUILD YOUR WEALTH BY SAVING TAXES

> *The government is aware of the heavy tax burden borne by Canadians and the costs this imposes on the economy. Accordingly, federal tax rates are not being raised.*
>
> *—1996 Federal Budget*

Really? What the last budget actually did was raise the level of personal taxation by $175 million in fiscal 1997–8, rising to $360 million more in 1998–9.

In fact, Ottawa's overall tax revenues are scheduled to rise dramatically—by $6 billion—within the next year. The good news is the federal deficit (the amount we spend each year more than we take in) will fall to $17 billion by the spring of 1998. The bad news is the country's debt (the total of our deficits) will rise to $619 billion from $578 billion last year. And it will cost a stunning $49 billion next year just to pay the interest on that debt.

A billion, by the way, is a thousand million. It looks like this: $1,000,000,000. If you spent $1,200 a day since Christ was born, you would not have hit a billion dollars yet. That wouldn't happen, actually, until July 2283.

Almost $50 billion a year in interest—to be borne by about 10 million taxpayers who contribute more into the system than they take out—the Canadian middle class, beasts of financial burden and the easiest of targets for the folks who write federal budgets.

This is precisely why Canadian taxes are not going down any time soon, and it is why tax planning is one of the most important things you can possibly do to help ensure your financial future. And nothing reduces taxes like an RRSP contribution.

Face it: The cost of living in this utopia is intense. If you make more than $60,000 a year, you are considered rich. That's when the top marginal tax rate clicks in, and suddenly you are giving over 53 cents of every dollar you earn. Compared with other countries, especially the United States, with whom our tax system competes, we are seriously out of step.

In the States, the top marginal tax rate is 39.6%, not 53%. And you don't pay that rate at an income level of just $60,000—instead, you start paying top buck when you are earning more than $256,500 a year (if single, or married and filing a joint return). So, it's clear: Tax planning is four or five times more important to Canadians than it is to Americans.

Our high taxes has resulted in a burgeoning underground economy that Revenue Canada this year will need $60 million more in taxes to combat.

And it has also spawned a new generation of tax cheats who are infatuated with the idea of sending their wealth offshore—many of them inspired by that little book *Take the Money and Run*. Efforts to counter that by Revenue Canada will cost us middle-class taxpayers an additional $60 million this fiscal year, and $70 million more in 1998–9.

Truth is, you don't need to be a tax cheat or evader to drastically reduce the amount of tax you pay. There are many ways to legally increase your income by decreasing your level of taxation.

> *Too many people pay more tax than the law requires. I was shocked when I became Minister of National Revenue in 1993 to see how many taxpayers overpaid. They missed obvious deductions and exemptions. They didn't use legal tax shelters like RRSPs. They didn't split their income with their spouses and children. They didn't make their mortgages tax-deductible. They didn't use any of these powerful RRSP strategies that can save thousands of dollars with just a couple of phone calls.*

A lot of wealthy Canadians know these strategies, and they use them. In fact, last year a record amount of money went into RRSPs—well over $20 billion—but the relative number of people contributing did not go up. It was just the same third of Canadians who have it figured out.

Too many others are walking away from their tax bills, changing names, declaring bankruptcy or working for cash. The Canadian middle class seems to be breaking in two—those who are cashing in RRSPs and those who are pumping them full.

More people declared bankruptcy in 1995 than ever before. And, in 1996, the personal failure rate at times was running at levels 40% higher.

As thousands more walk away from their tax obligations, it leaves a dwindling number of middle-class people to pay the freight. Now just 30% of Canadian families pay more than 62% of all taxes.

So, the simplest survival rule for 1997 and beyond is this: It's far easier to save money than to make money.

And this is what the RRSP—North America's best tax shelter—is all about.

The amount of money you will save on your 1996 taxes by making an RRSP contribution by March 1, 1997, depends on how much money you put in, and your marginal tax rate.

The marginal rate is determined by the combination of federal and provincial income taxes where you live, and varies slightly from province to province. Here is how Canadians are taxed federally.

FEDERAL TAX RATES

Income level	Tax rate	Including surtax
$29,590 or less	17%	17.5%
$29,591 to $59,180	26%	26.8%
$59,181 to $62,195	29%	29.9%
Above $62,196	29%	31.3%

Added to this are provincial income taxes, which are levied as a percentage of federal tax payable. The rates range from a low of 45% in the Northwest Territories to a high of 69% in Newfoundland. In addition, most provinces have high income surtaxes, and three—Alberta, Manitoba and Saskatchewan—also impose flat taxes. As a result, the maximum combined tax rates range from 44.3% in the Northwest Territories to a high of 54.1% in British Columbia.

> *To calculate your tax reduction, simply multiply the amount you can contribute to your RRSP by your marginal tax rate.*

For example, if you live in Nova Scotia, and had taxable income in 1996 of $68,000, and could make the maximum RRSP contribution of $12,240, this is how to determine your refund:

$$\$12,240 \times 48.5\% = \$5,936$$

If you live in British Columbia and last year had a taxable income of $35,000, and made the maximum allowance contribution of $6,300, this would be your refund:

$$\$6,300 \times 40.4\% = \$2,545$$

You can easily see that the current system clearly favours people with higher incomes, because the RRSP contribution reduces taxable income, and therefore the tax payable. The more money you make, the higher your tax bracket. And the higher the tax bracket you are in, the more you save by making a contribution.

There is the strong possibility this may change in the future, with Ottawa going to a system of tax credits which would address the idea some have that wealthier Canadians are getting a disproportionate RRSP break. But the system as it is today also recognizes the fact that upper-income Canadians shoulder a massive amount of the tax burden.

The most significant thing upper-middle-class tax-payers can do to increase their family incomes— freeing up tens of thousands of dollars to invest in today's booming financial markets—is to maximize annual RRSP contributions.

Start this year, this month, this week. The sooner the money is put into the plan, the faster it will compound. And recognize that basic investing should start inside the RRSP bubble. If you have $10,000 to invest in mutual funds, first put it inside a self-directed RRSP. That will earn you a tax refund of $4,000 to $5,000. Now you have thousands more to put into funds, both inside and outside the retirement savings plan. Next year you can use a portion of your contribution room to move the funds outside the RRSP into it—and, just for doing that, you will receive another tax-rebate cheque of about $2,000.

Meanwhile your funds should give you double-digit annual returns. So, one year after investing $10,000 in a self-directed RRSP, you will have about $17,000 in assets.

How much would your salary have to be increased to take home an extra $7,000 this year? In the top tax bracket in Ontario, you'd need a raise of more than $14,000—and there aren't too many of those around these days.

The tables below give you combined federal and provincial income-tax rates, by province, so you can calculate the exact tax savings your 1996 RRSP contribution will yield. They will also help you decide if it makes more sense to work harder to earn more income, or concentrate on earning investment income—interest, capital gain or dividend, in descending order of most heavily taxed.

Five provinces announced income-tax cuts in 1996: Ontario, British Columbia, Saskatchewan, Nova Scotia and Alberta. The biggest tax cut comes in Ontario, where the provincial rate will be reduced from 58% of federal tax to 50%—the first in a series of cuts promised by the Mike Harris government over three years.

If you live in Ontario and are in the top tax bracket, that means an RRSP contribution will be worth more to you in tax savings than it will be in the future. So, it makes sense to catch up on missed contributions and to make your 1997 contribution now.

The tax tables here are for taxable, not gross, income, and do not reflect any clawbacks, while assuming employment-insurance and CPP or QPP premiums are paid.

1996 PERSONAL INCOME TAX RATES (%)

Combined federal and provincial

Source: KPMG

1996 taxable income	$6,750–29,590	$29,591–35,400	$35,401–39,000	$39,001–59,180	$59,181–63,392	$63,393–& over
British Columbia (1)						
Salary	24.8	38.8	39.5	40.3/44.4	49.5	50.9/54.2
Interest	26.4	40.3	40.3	40.3/44.4	49.5	50.9/54.2
Dividends	7.1	24.5	24.5	24.5/27.0	33.4	34.4/36.6
Capital Gains	19.8	30.2	30.2	30.2/33.3	37.1	38.2/40.6
Alberta (2)						
Salary	24.3	37.7	38.4	39.1/40.1	44.6	46.1
Interest	25.8	39.1	39.1	39.1/40.1	44.6	46.1
Dividends	7.4	24.1	24.1	24.1/24.7	30.4	31.4
Capital Gains	19.3	29.3	29.3	29.3/30.0	33.5	34.6
Saskatchewan (3)						
Salary	27.5	41.7	42.5	43.3/45.5	50.5	52.0
Interest	29.1	43.3	43.3	43.3/45.5	50.5	52.0

1996 PERSONAL INCOME TAX RATES (%) continued
Combined federal and provincial

Dividends	10.0	27.8	27.8	27.8/29.3	35.5	36.5
Capital Gains	21.8	32.5	32.5	32.5/34.2	37.9	39.0
Manitoba (4)						
Salary	26.8	40.8/42.8	43.5	44.3	49.0	50.4
Interest	28.4	42.3/44.3	44.3	44.3	49.0	50.4
Dividends	9.6	27.0/29.5	29.5	29.5	35.4	36.3
Capital Gains	21.3	31.7/33.2	33.2	33.2	36.7	37.8
Ontario (5)						
Salary	25.5	39.8	40.5	41.3/44.3	49.4	50.8/52.9
Interest	27.0	41.3	41.3	41.3/44.3	49.4	50.8/52.9
Dividends	7.3	25.2	25.2	25.2/27.0	33.3	34.3/35.7
Capital Gains	20.3	31.0	31.0	31.0/33.2	37.0	38.1/39.7
New Brunswick (6)						
Salary	26.8	41.8	42.6	43.4	48.8	49.9/51.4
Interest	28.4	43.4	43.4	43.4	48.4	49.9/51.4
Dividends	7.7	26.4	26.4	32.7	32.7	33.7/34.7
Capital Gains	21.3	32.6	32.6	32.6	36.3	37.4/38.5

Nova Scotia (7)

Salary	26.0	40.7	41.4	42.3	47.1	48.6/50.3
Interest	27.6	42.3	42.3	42.3	47.1	48.6/50.3
Dividends	7.5	25.7	25.7	25.7	31.8	32.8/34.0
Capital Gains	20.7	31.7	31.7	31.7	35.3	36.4/37.7

Prince Edward Island (8)

Salary	26.0	40.7	41.4	42.3	47.1	48.6/50.3
Interest	27.6	42.3	42.3	42.3	47.1	48.6/50.3
Dividends	7.5	25.7	25.7	25.7	31.8	32.8/34.0
Capital Gains	20.7	31.7	31.7	31.7	35.3	36.4/37.7

Newfoundland (9)

Salary	27.6	43.0	43.9	44.7	49.9/51.9	53.3
Interest	29.2	44.7	44.7	44.7/46.5	51.9	53.3
Dividends	7.9	27.2	27.2	27.2/28.3	35.0	36.0
Capital Gains	21.9	33.5	33.5	33.5/34.9	38.9	40.0

Yukon (10)

Salary	24.5	38.3	39.0	39.8	44.4/45.1	46.6
Interest	26.0	39.8	39.8	39.8	44.4/45.1	46.6
Dividends	7.0	24.2	24.2	24.2	30.0/31.0	31.4
Capital Gains	19.5	29.8	29.8	29.8	33.3/33.8	34.9

1996 PERSONAL INCOME TAX RATES (%) continued

Combined federal and provincial

Northwest Territories (10)

Salary	23.7	37.0	37.7	38.5	42.9	44.4
Interest	25.2	38.5	38.5	38.5	42.9	44.4
Dividends	6.8	23.5	23.4	23.4	29.0	30.0
Capital Gains	18.9	28.9	28.9	28.9	32.2	33.3

Secondary rate thresholds by province:

1. $55,000 and $79,410 for salary; $53,664 and $78,208 for investment income
2. $45,384 for salary and $44,050 for investment income
3. $40,360 for salary and $39,205 for investment income
4. Threshold is $30,000
5. $52,269 and $67,300 for salary, $50,937 and $66,108 for investment income.
6. $93,024 for salary and $91,830 for investment income
7. $78,241 for salary and $77,043 for investment income.
8. $92,731 for salary and $91,532 for investment income
9. $59,770 for salary and $58,500 for investment income
10. $61,666 for salary and $60,469 for investment income

1996 PERSONAL INCOME TAX RATES (%)
continued

Combined federal and provincial rates for Quebec

On Salary

Taxable Income	Rate
$6,750–8,780	13.9
$8,781–14,000	32.1
$14,001–23,000	34.1
$23,001–29,590	36.2
$29,591–32,535	44.0
$32,536–35,400	45.0
$35,401–39,000	46.0
$39,001–50,000	46.5
$50,001–54,395	48.2
$54,396–59,180	48.9
$59,181–63,400	51.5
$63,401 and over	52.9

On Investment Income

Taxable Income	Interest	Dividends	Capital Gains
$6,459–8,349	14.7	4.0	11.0
$8,350–14,000	34.1	16.9	25.6
$14,001–23,000	36.1	19.4	27.1
$23,001–29,590	38.2	22.0	28.6
$29,591–31,000	46.0	31.7	34.5
$31,001–50,000	47.1	32.6	35.3
$50,001–52,625	48.2	34.0	36.1
$52,626–59,180	48.9	34.5	36.7
$59,181–62,195	51.5	37.7	38.6
$62,196 and over	52.9	38.7	39.7

YOUR MORTGAGE VERSUS YOUR RRSP: NO CONTEST

It's a constant question at financial seminars. Invariably somebody—usually a younger person—will stand up and ask if it's better to build up an RRSP or pay down a mortgage.

THE GLOBE AND MAIL

More Canadians losing homes

Soaring foreclosure rate reflects big debt loads, poor real-estate market, huge job losses

BY SUSAN BOURETTE
The Globe and Mail

Canadians are losing their homes

pace not seen for a decade. The numbers do not include mortgages not insured under the federal

have defaulted on their mortgages. "It's been a continuous stream of people since the reces-

CMHC insures high-ratio mortgages in which the buyer provides less than a 25-per-cent

analyst based in Alberta, said provincial mortgage defaults are concentrated in Edmonton.

Get used to it. The days of real assets are ending. The long-term outlook for residential real estate—especially the kind that was hot in the Eighties—is bleak.

Source: *The Globe and Mail*

Most financial advisers fudge on the issue, saying, on the one hand, mortgage debt is expensive and non-deductible, and the longer you have a home loan, the more interest you will pay. That's all true.

On the other hand, the more years you have money compounding tax-free within an RRSP, the greater the chances you will retire comfortable, if not wealthy. Also a valid point. And there are some advisers who live by computer spreadsheets and handy formulas—to them it makes sense to pay down the mortgage first if the loan rate is 2% higher than what the investments in your RRSP are earning.

The final school of thought is this: Make your maximum RRSP contribution every year and then use the tax-refund cheque to pay down the mortgage principal. That makes a lot of sense, and it will work. But it's slow.

I have a better strategy, and it is rooted in the firm belief residential real estate has no long-term future.

> *You should be investing in residential real estate only during the first half of your life, more as a forced-savings plan than as a way to build capital. In the second half of your life, sell or use the equity through leverage.*

I have recently detailed, in my book *2015: After the Boom*, why real estate, especially residential real estate, faces a steady, relentless erosion of value. The signs are all around us—the Nineties to date have been cruel to homeowners, reducing the net worth of millions of people through falling prices, rising maintenance costs and vicious property taxes.

The price of an average resale home in the country's largest market, Toronto, hit $280,000 in the autumn of 1989. It ranged lower by 31%, to hit $193,000 in February 1996, before bouncing higher in the real-estate boomlet I predicted a year earlier was going to take place as the result of pent-up demand and cheap mortgage rates. But it was a false market, based on first-time buyers giving some scared Baby Boomers a chance to bail out. The march downwards will continue.

Why is this happening?

Because all over the industrialized world, and especially in Canada, where we have a rapidly aging population, there is a trend away from real assets and towards financial assets. Real estate is a real asset. RRSPs with mutual funds stuffed in them are financial assets.

> *The unfortunate part is that most Canadians have most of their wealth in the wrong type of assets—namely, their homes.*

The rise of financial assets in the coming decade—a trend that will explode higher after the millennium—will serve only to drive the value of real assets lower. Already, with $3 trillion invested in mutual funds,

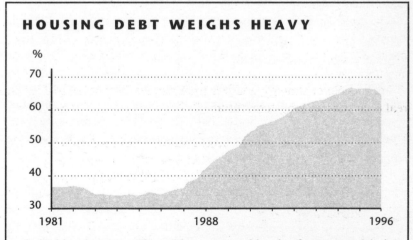

HOUSING DEBT WEIGHS HEAVY

A double whammy: After taking on record levels of mortgage debt in the Eighties to finance inflated real estate, housing values plunged in the Nineties, leaving consumers with falling equity and huge liabilities. Things will likely get worse.

Source: *The Financial Post*

American investors have shifted a large portion of what used to be home equity into stocks and bonds and other securities.

Demand for bricks and mortar will decline. That doesn't mean real estate is dead—but it is changing. Demographics will drastically shrink the number of potential buyers. Baby Boomers hitting 50 after the year 2000 will start to become obsessed with the need to earn double-digit rates of return on their RRSPs, and realize they are sitting on tens or hundreds of thousands of dollars in their homes, earning them zero, or even negative returns. Then it will be a race to see who can get out of residential real estate the fastest, before the value of some kinds of real estate—large, suburban homes, for example—simply evaporates.

Why? Because there will not be the universe of buyers there to maintain those values.

• Bummed out by uncertainty about their own employment prospects and the likelihood they will face an economic depression in the middle of their working lives, Generation Xers are in no mood to take on massive mortgage debt.

• Immigration is a bright spot in markets like Vancouver, but many immigrant families tend to be larger and multigenerational, with the move to individual real estate much slower.

• And the Baby Boomers—all 9 million of them—generally are living in the largest homes of their lives, unlikely to move up, and just about certain to move down.

So, why would you invest in real estate right now?

Well, as a young person, buying a starter home, it's a way to build up some equity in the kind of house that will have a better resale future—a townhome or condo or bungalow near services that will appeal to aging Boomers in another decade.

Buying is also a way to stabilize your housing costs, especially when mortgage rates are as low as they've been in the past couple of years. And in places like Ontario, where government rent controls will be ended, owning gives some assurance that you know what monthly costs will be.

But for middle-aged people and older, real estate is a potential financial sinkhole. You should be getting at least some of your equity out, and into the financial assets that have a gleaming future. Remember: You needn't sell your home if you don't want to—just don't have so much of your net worth in one, vulnerable asset.

*With the trend from real assets to financial assets,
real estate has a dark future. In a decade, many houses
will not be worth the mortgages placed upon them.
But tax-sheltered funds, bonds and stocks will explode
in value. Mortgage or RRSP? There is no contest.*

So the strategy is this: Make the maximum RRSP contribution, no matter what your age. Then if you are a younger homeowner, you can apply the tax refund to the mortgage to pay it off in the shortest possible time—but don't stop there. Use the other techniques at your disposal, like weekly payments, which can shave more than a decade from the time it takes to retire a mortgage.

Remember these truths:

- Younger investors can afford to take on a lot more risk than older ones. So, first-time home buyers who put money into RRSPs should be investing that cash through a self-directed plan into growth assets—equity-based mutual funds; international growth funds; emerging market, Asian and Latin funds, for example.

  Remember that $100,000 put into Templeton Growth 20 years ago grew into well over $2 million. Cash put into Fidelity Growth America Fund more than doubled in just 5 years. And these are not considered to be the riskiest of funds, by any means.

  Time is on the side of the young investor, and time always defeats risk. The farther from retirement you are, the more valuable are your RRSP contributions because of tax-free compounding. Will $100,000 equity in your house grow into $2 million two decades from now? Actually, I think you'll be lucky to get your money out, with more than a small premium for inflation.

- Always remember that Canadians have too much of their personal wealth tied up in their houses. The strategy worked for most of the time since the Second World War—rising real-estate values meant a lot of people didn't have to save and plan for retirement. (Besides "retirement" 20 years ago lasted for 8 or 10 years. Now it can be 30.)

  But as the Nineties end, you must diversify your assets, shifting wealth until, approaching middle age, you have at least half your net worth outside your house, and then increase that as you near retirement.

  It is a shocking reality that almost 60% of Canadians who have paid off the mortgage don't have an RRSP!

- Being a real asset, instead of a financial one, real estate is illiquid. That means you can't cash it in unless you persuade somebody else to buy it from you.

   Most people forget this, and end up selling at the wrong time, because they are forced to sell by circumstances. As in the instance of a marriage breakdown, when the family home has to be dumped fast—and usually at a firesale price.

   Or it can be the result of age and inaction—people growing old, not doing what they should, when they should, and then being faced with a crisis when sickness strikes. I have seen this firsthand in my own family, and I do not wish the experience on anyone. Real estate is not an appropriate asset for most seniors. Period. It can end up destroying wealth—trapping it in bricks and mortar, and then eating it up in maintenance, insurance, taxes and utilities.

   > *Buy a house when you're young. Take the equity out and use it to build wealth when you're middle-aged. Dump it before you grow old.*

- After you are 40, whether your house is paid for or not, take your RRSP tax refunds and plough them back into financial assets. Remember—every year you age, your assets have a shorter time to grow. You will be farther ahead to have them accumulate than you will to make the equity in your home larger. After all, if residential real estate declines in value between now and retirement (a safe bet for most people over 40), the loss will not come off the mortgage you owe—it stays constant. It will all come off the equity.

- But if you do pay off your mortgage, make sure you keep on writing monthly cheques of the same size—this time not to the bank or trust company, but into your RRSP.

   Take advantage of the financial discipline that mortgage taught you—setting aside enough each month to meet an important obligation. I'm sure your RRSP funds, properly invested, will turn out to be far more important in your life than paying off that mortgage ever was.

- If you are in your thirties, or more probably in your forties, and you have built up equity in your home, it's time to start using it.

   There are several ways of doing this, but one of the easiest is to call up the bank and get a home-equity loan—a form of mortgage that will give you cash to invest in financial assets, which you can slide into your RRSP as "contributions in kind" over future years.

And why would you mortgage your home after working so hard to pay it off?

First, remember—residential real estate has no long-term future. You do not want to be stuck with an expensive asset, you can't sell unless you throw away a pile of equity. Ten or 15 years from now many Canadians will wake up to that reality.

Second, the interest you pay on a home-equity loan is tax-deductible—because this is an investment loan. If you are in the 54% tax bracket, for example, you simply write off 54% of the interest on your annual tax return. Of course, this dramatically lowers the actual cost of borrowing. Here's an example:

USING YOUR EQUITY
The true costs of a home-equity loan used for investment purposes

Equity loan rate:	7%
Your tax rate:	54%
Rate write-off:	3.78%
Actual, after-tax loan rate:	3.2%

Where else could you find $50,000 or $100,000 with one phone call at the effective after-tax rate of about 3%? By using your home equity and then investing the money in quality, mutual funds that track stock-market performance, you will see the money that used to be earning zero in your house suddenly making double-digit returns.

Is this a dangerous strategy?

Some say yes. And when I proffered this strategy first in *2015: After the Boom*, there were critics and sceptics who had a hard time surrendering their Eighties inflationary notions that real estate is a secure and growing storehouse of wealth, and that the stock market is not the place any careful Canadian invests.

That didn't surprise me. It's that attitude that will keep many Canadians dependent in their old age on the dwindling crumbs of support offered by a bankrupt government. They may be living in paid-up houses all right, but they may also have to choose between heating them or eating.

The myth of stock market risks

History shows me there is virtually no risk in the stock market, so long as an investor is in it for the long term and does not try to pick individual companies to invest in. Certainly, given the fact that the North American economy is gaining speed and will be powered further by demographics (100 million Baby Boomers entering their peak income years across North America) and tax cuts (starting in the United States, likely in 1998), stocks are a rising tide that can lift family wealth higher while real estate puts it at risk.

Yes, we are in an era when it is possible to buy high, and sell higher—much higher. Those who will lose are the ones standing on the sidelines, wealth parked in houses and GICs, wringing their hands and warning that one day the Dow Industrial Index could fall 1,000 points, or maybe even 1,500!

Of course it could, and it probably will. But smart investors knew it was not the end of the world when the equivalent happened on October 19, 1987—Black Monday. In hindsight, it turned out to be a heck of a buying opportunity, which is exactly what the next dump will be.

Meanwhile, real estate has already seen its top. And it was an amazing coincidence that the housing market peaked on about the same day the stock market crashed. Or was it?

WHAT KIND OF RRSP IS RIGHT FOR YOU?

I wrote earlier most people think an RRSP is a thing, a product—an investment on its own—and they believe it always earns interest. Wrong.

That is the case only when somebody—through choice or, usually, ignorance—decides to throw away the awesome flexibility and potential that RRSP rules allow, and lets his or her money just sit in a no-risk, low-yield savings account or debt security like a GIC.

Sure, this is appropriate for some people, who live in fear of taking any risk at all—typically folks now at retirement age who grew up remembering the Depression, which was caused in part by stock-market speculation. They want their money guaranteed, and rules have been put into place to do just that—ensuring nobody will lose less than $60,000 in a GIC issued by a bank, broker, trust or credit union that's a member of the Canada Deposit Insurance Corporation.

Although the GIC-type RRSP is the preferred choice of most Canadians, thank goodness things are starting to change. Our aging population is simply going to run out of private retirement funds if it relies on interest-bearing securities like savings accounts and guaranteed investment certificates. And this is certainly not appropriate for young people starting out on their investments, or middle-aged people like me who have just 20 years left to maximize retirement assets.

First, realize you have a choice of RRSP bubbles—boring, better and best—and three different levels of risk—none, some and as-much-as-you-want. Here's how they compare:

The boring ones

At the bottom of the RRSP food chain are plans that put your money into either deposit accounts or guaranteed investment certificates. Savings RRSPs pay you a ridiculously low rate of interest that moves up and down with the prime, just like the rate you have on your daily-interest chequing or savings account (have you checked that lately?).

The advantages are that it is safe, in the sense the money on deposit will not go down. And you will be guaranteed up to $60,000 from Ottawa if your financial institution goes belly-up.

But the overriding danger is your savings will probably not even rise as much as inflation does, meaning you are actually suffering a

Source: *The Financial Post*

loss in the purchasing power of your retirement nest egg. That is definitely not cool.

It is my view that interest rates across the Western world will remain low for a long time to come—at least a decade—thanks to an aging population, low inflation and declining government deficits. So, opening a savings RRSP is not in the cards for most of us.

One step up (but a small one) is the RRSP that puts your money in a GIC. It's still the most popular, but the low rates of the 1990s are changing investment habits fast.

What is a GIC? It stands for "guaranteed investment certificate" and, most commonly, it works like this: You give the bank $5,000 for five years and it agrees to pay you, say, 6.5% on that money in each of those years. Then the bank turns around, pools your $5,000 with the investments of other people and lends $50,000 out in the form of a five-year mortgage at 8.5%.

That's one way banks make money, and you earn 6.5%—guaranteed, just like the homeowner is guaranteed his or her mortgage rate will not rise over the same period.

So, a fixed rate is one advantage, and the GIC is again insured to the $60,000 limit. You know exactly how much money the investment will earn, and within an RRSP the interest compounds tax-free.

But the advantages are also the drawbacks. In return for a fixed rate of return, you will get a low rate. And in return for the time guarantee, you give up cashability and flexibility. The GIC cannot be cashed in and, if rates rise, you don't enjoy any of the increase. There is no potential for growth, or capital gain and, as with a savings-type RRSP, your asset growth is not protected from the ravages of inflation, even moderate inflation.

These are all heavy prices to pay for the premium of no risk.

As I argue elsewhere in this book, the greatest risk facing most Canadians today is not losing money in a bad investment; rather, it's outliving the money you've got. Assets locked into a low-yield savings or GIC RRSPs will add significantly to that larger risk.

> *TIP: Here's a far better alternative to a GIC—one that offers a greater rate of return and even less risk than a GIC, along with the potential for a capital gain, and even the ability to cash it before maturity: government strip bonds. These are bonds issued by the federal and provincial governments,*

stripped of interest, so they are bought at a deep discount to face value. The principal is guaranteed by the government, no matter what the value, so there is no risk. And you can sell them at any time. Finally, if interest rates keep going down (which I believe will happen), the bonds become more valuable, giving you a capital gain. So, why would anyone go for a GIC when this kind of a deal is available? Simply because they don't know about them, or where to buy them.

For complete details read the section "Wealth without risk: Strip bonds" in Chapter 5.

There are many different kinds of GICs now available in the marketplace, as the banks and trusts try to compete with much more attractive investments. They like to lend money as GICs, because it is so convenient to match up these deposits with the mortgage loans they make to homeowners. And because low interest rates have disillusioned a growing number of people who usually invested in them, they've come up with these alternatives.

Almost all of these new-wave GICs are marketed exclusively in the first couple of months of a new year, so watch for them in January and February 1997. Some others come out in the fall, just when the federal government is pushing its Canada Savings Bonds, to compete with them.

Most are, frankly, gimmicks. Sure, you can improve by a little the rate of return you might enjoy on a traditional GIC, but not by much. Certainly, in my view, you are better off 10 times out of 10 investing in mutual funds or government bonds. But for a good portion of the population, life begins and ends with GICs, and for them even these small refinements are big news. So, here are some of the newer GICs to look out for this year.

- *For those who think interest rates will be lower in a year's time:* Extendible GICs are available. Typically, you lock your money up for a year, then have the right to extend the one-year rate for another year. Are rates going down? Likely not, certainly not in the long-term. So this is of dubious value.

- *For those who normally buy Canada Savings Bonds:* Redeemable GICs are on sale for a short period when CSBs are marketed. They are just like savings bonds—you can cash them in after a few months and they'll pay a slightly higher rate of return. And the advantages are the same as for CSBs—a place to park cash for a while and earn more than in a bank savings account. For long-term investment, though, forget it.

• *For those who wish interest rates would go up:* You can buy escalating GICs that give the appearance of high rates.

In 1996, for example, Canada Trust brought out a GIC with an escalating rate that went all the way up to 10% after seven years. But here's the rub: The only true way to compare these with other GICs is to look at the blended rate—that is, the average rate of return over all the years the GIC is locked in. That, you will almost always discover, is very close to the rate paid by a traditional investment certificate.

You are, of course, locked into this investment for years and, if it is held outside your RRSP (a very bad idea), you are taxed on the blended rate—which will be higher in the early years than the rate you are actually getting.

• *For people who want the sizzle of stock markets, but who are wimps:* Market index–related GICs increase the rate of return as stocks rise in value.

Sounds good, but be careful. Many of these are just marketing creations and, in general, the premium you receive is tiny. The idea is to guarantee investors a minimum rate over a fixed period of time—usually a rate less than with traditional GICs of the same duration. Then you get extra if the TSE 300 or the TSE 35 index of the Standard and Poor's 500 index rises (those are all measures of stock-market activity).

> **TIP: You are far better off to invest in the stock market directly through equity-based mutual funds. These are professionally managed funds that spread investors' risk by investing in scores of various stocks, in Canada, North America or around the world. Not only will you benefit from the long-term growth of the stock market, but you will be paid income in the form of capital gains, not interest. So, if the funds are ever held outside your RRSP, the income they generate will have much less tax exposure.**

A better alternative—Mutual-fund RRSPs

Mutual funds are growing so rapidly in popularity because they are giving most investors the double-digit rates of return they want, and need, to build retirement assets. Canadians now have more than $160 billion in funds, while Americans have more than $3 trillion—about double our investment on a per-capita basis.

All of the mutual-fund companies will get you set up with a fund RRSP, or you can deal with your financial adviser. The trick here is to make an educated decision about what kind of funds you want to invest in. There are well over 1,000 to choose from, and in many different categories—a confusing array, indeed. When I am asked how I pick my own mutual funds, my answer is always a surprise: I write a cheque to my financial planner and tell him to pick. After all, he's the pro. He's supposed to spend his days studying all this. So far, I have no complaints—my mutual funds went up last year, on average, 15.1%. I'm not greedy. That's enough.

If I were to pick my own funds, at my age (47), the obvious choice would be growth funds—those that are based on the performance of the stock market. Over the balance of the next 20 years, for many reasons (including falling interest rates, rising corporate profits, a U.S. tax cut, booming trade, low inflation and the influence of the Baby Boomers), stock markets will boom. It is reasonable to expect your funds will double in value, tax-free within your RRSP—every five or six years.

But if you want less risk (although I believe investing long-term in the market is virtually free of risk), then you can put your money into fixed-income funds that invest in bonds (government and corporate) as well as mortgages.

And if you can't decide, or want some growth as well as fixed-income security, there are balanced funds to consider. They spread their assets among both categories.

All of these funds will give you professional management and more diversification than you could ever get yourself. They have a vastly higher potential for growth than any kind of GIC, but, of course, unlike a GIC, the returns are not guaranteed. There is more risk.

There is also usually more cost—most funds come with commissions attached, typically a few percentage points of the amount invested. Some funds charge the commission (called a "load") upfront, when you buy it; others charge you when fund units are cashed in.

The thought of paying a commission drives many people into the arms of no-load funds, like Altamira, T-D Green Line or Scudder, to name a few. This is fine for people who want to save a few bucks, and many of the funds these companies manage have excellent track records, but for me it is really a false economy.

Most no-load funds are also no-help funds. You do not get to access the expertise of a financial adviser to guide you into the right fund purchase. In fact, the consultant on the other end of the no-load company phone line is typically a recent college graduate making $30,000 and still living with Mom. I know—I've seen them. And that's not exactly the person I want to be making decisions about my retirement

The best RRSPs: Self-directed

Here is the way an RRSP should really work—the way you can take maximum advantage of all the strategies that I am presenting in this book and that the rules currently allow.

A self-directed RRSP is nothing more than a bubble that shelters whatever is inside from tax. It's not run by the bank, like a GIC RRSP. And it's not run by a mutual-fund company. Instead, it is run by you. But, one hopes, you have the wisdom to have the plan administered by a financial planner whose advice you trust.

It will cost you between $100 and $300 a year in administration fees to a financial institution, or a broker, to run a self-directed RRSP. Until the last federal budget, that fee was tax-deductible, but no longer. As well, there will be fees to pay as you transfer your existing RRSP assets into a self-directed plan. Still, this is a cheap way to get flexibility and control.

You can put any qualifying investment you want in a self-directed plan. You can buy and sell various assets and move them around within the bubble. The level of risk and the potential for growth are yours alone to determine.

But if you are working with a good adviser, and putting assets in the right places, like quality, equity-based mutual funds, the up-side can be great.

You need only one self-directed plan. In fact, all of your tax-sheltered retirement assets should be consolidated within a single self-directed plan. That way they can be managed in harmony, and you will also keep administrative fees to a minimum.

How do you start a self-directed plan?

It's as simple as sitting down with your adviser, broker or banker and filling out some forms. You can do this when you make your annual RRSP contribution; or you can open the plan and then transfer in either assets you already own (mutual funds, stocks, GICs, CSBs, etc.), or existing RRSPs at other institutions.

The transfer fee can be as low as $25 or as high as $100, but don't fret about it. The advantages of having all your retirement assets in one plan will far outweigh the one-time transfer costs. Be aware, however, that transferring assets from an existing bank or trust can be a frustrating experience, taking weeks, even months.

As these institutions are in fierce competition for your money, they are loath to give it up. Notify them as early as possible that a maturing GIC or term deposit will be transferred, then make sure you have a good paper trail.

To do the transfer, fill out a T-2033 form (your broker, adviser or banker has it) and have it sent to where the funds are. This will allow them to be sent to your self-directed plan without any taxes being deducted. If you don't do this, you could run the risk of your RRSP simply being collapsed, and becoming fully taxable. Clearly a bad idea.

Make arrangements to go to the bank itself to pick up a cashier's or certified cheque for the amount, then take it directly to where your self-directed plan is being administered.

Now, what do you put in your self-administered RRSP?

The answer depends on your age, assets, tolerance for risk, the status of your spouse and several other factors. In general, the younger you are, the more heavily invested you should be in stocks and equity mutual funds. As you age, the amount of fixed-income should rise.

And, as a general rule of thumb, your RRSP assets should be slightly more conservatively managed than assets you hold outside the plan. Why? Because their tax-free status simply means they will perform better, and you do not need to take as much risk to get the same rate of return.

Here's an example. As I write this, here are the asset summaries of my own self-directed RRSP and my Canadian-dollar account:

GARTH TURNER'S ACCOUNTS

Self-directed RRSP		Canadian-dollar account	
Cash	0%	Cash	0%
Fixed Income	55%	Fixed Income	39%
Mutual Funds	25%	Mutual Funds	42%
Foreign Securities	20%	Equities	19%
Total	100%	Total	100%

OOH-LA-LA: MAXING YOUR
FOREIGN CONTENT

*We have suffered a tangible loss of economic
sovereignty.*

—*Department of Finance*

Canada is a great country, but you sure don't want to have all your
wealth in Canadian dollars.

The loonie could tank in 1997 thanks to Lucien Bouchard and the
re-emerging crisis surrounding the future of Quebec and the rest of the
country. History has shown us that the dollar falls, short-term interest
rates spike higher, and financial assets melt every time the world starts
hearing from the separatists. There is every reason to believe it's going
to happen again.

Bouchard, of course, almost won the vote on October 30, 1995.
Now, as premier of Quebec, he is in a powerful position to take another run at it. I hope some accommodation is found to keep Canada
whole, but there is still a strong possibility this will be another referendum year.

Investors who realize that should take action. The dollar may well
test its all-time low of 69 cents, and take some time to improve after
that. If you have all your wealth in Canadian currency, you will lose
purchasing power as interest rates rise—unless you have assets to offset that, assets which rise in value when the dollar falls. In other words,
foreign assets, things denominated in other kinds of money.

Then there's the debt.

For only the second time in Canadian history, federal government
debt equals 100% of the country's total output. Yes, the first time was
in 1946, after billions had been spent building the tanks and bombers
that won the Second World War. No war now—just the steady piling-
on of annual deficits as governments continue to spend more than they
take in in tax.

Today national savings are more than wiped out by those deficits.
The net domestic savings rate has been reduced to zero, compared with
an average rate of 7% in the 1980s, and 9.5% in the 1970s.

With all our savings gone through deficits, we have to borrow more
and more money abroad. That has raised our external debt to $350 bil-
lion and, at 45% of the economy, that is the highest foreign-debt ratio
in the world.

In fact, we are so deep in the debt soup that, the federal Department of Finance admits, "we have suffered a tangible loss of economic sovereignty."

The consequences for all of us as investors are stark. We are completely vulnerable to interest-rate swings outside our borders, and more susceptible to global financial gyrations than ever before, and than the people of almost any other nation.

Every twelve months, we ship an average of $29 billion in Canadian currency out of the country and into the pockets of American, German, Japanese and other bondholders in the form of interest. That's money that does not come back—a massive transfer of wealth from you and me.

This, of course, is fiscal insanity. It screams for political attention. But, to date, nobody in power in Ottawa has talked seriously about the need for laws to ensure the federal budget is balanced. If Finance Minister Paul Martin sticks to his present budget projections—achieving a deficit equal to 2% of the economy—then our current federal debt of more than $550 billion will rise to $800 billion within five years. And the interest payments will go up just as fast.

> *Now, you may not be able to change this, but you certainly can shield yourself from the debt disaster that is looming out there someplace beyond the year 2015. And your RRSP is the place to start.*

You are allowed 20% of the assets in your RRSP to be held as foreign content. That is not nearly enough, but it's what we have to live with for now. Ottawa has wrongly dictated that most retirement money be invested in Canada—a rule that is not needed, and in fact hurts investment in this country by signalling to foreigners that our markets require this measure of coddling.

This restriction also means too many people will have too much of their wealth in a currency that is too much at risk. So, by all means, do not restrict your foreign-currency investments to what's in your RRSP. You can diversify outside your RRSP, as well as within it, in several ways:

• Buy into global mutual funds. They take your Canadian dollars and make investments denominated in foreign currency, while the fund unit price stays in Canadian currency. That means if the loonie falls, the relative worth of the foreign-currency holdings rises, which buoys the fund unit price, protecting you.

Besides, with Canadian markets representing only 3% of those around the world, it just makes sense to be spreading your assets around.

* Or you can invest in Canadian companies that will give you an income stream in other currencies. For example, after the 1995 referendum, when it became clear Lucien Bouchard would succeed Jacques Parizeau and become premier of Quebec, setting the stage for another referendum, I rebalanced my portfolio to Bouchard-proof it.

    One of my purchases was preferred shares of the Royal Bank, which was poised to announce record profits. But the best part is that the bank pays me dividends on those shares in U.S. dollars.

* And if you want the security of fixed-income investments, you can always buy government bonds, which are also denominated in other currencies.

    These bonds are issued by governments like Alberta's and British Columbia's or by Crown corporations like Ontario Hydro, and they will pay you interest in German marks or Japanese yen. And there is no need to convert your Canadian dollars into those currencies when you make the bond purchase.

Now, inside your RRSP, here is how the 20% foreign content rule works:

You are allowed up to 20% of the "book value" of your RRSP assets to be foreign—book value means the price you originally paid, not the market value, which is what the assets are worth today. The book value also includes all fees or commissions you had to pay to acquire those assets, like brokerage fees and front-end-load commissions on mutual funds.

If your self-administered RRSP is managed by a professional financial adviser or broker (and it should be), then you will get a regular accounting of the percentage of foreign content. Just make sure it hovers around 19%, giving a little flexibility.

If you are taking on the task of running your own RRSP, then the monitoring is up to you. Here's what to remember:

* It's the book value that matters, not the market value. So if your global mutual funds rise in value, and all of a sudden amount to $3,000 of your $10,000 RRSP, don't worry. Your book value has not changed.

- However, if the makeup of your RRSP changes, you could have a problem. For example, if the value of a GIC collapsed (remember Confederation Life?), then the proportion of your foreign content would rise, even though your global mutual funds might not have. Then, if the fund book value exceeds 20% of your reduced RRSP, you need to take action.

- Revenue Canada will impose a penalty on your RRSP if the foreign content stays above 20%. That penalty will be 1% a month on the excess—and it needs to be paid in precious RRSP-sheltered dollars.

If this happens, then you must sell enough of the foreign assets to get back onside, deposit more assets into your plan (if you have the contribution room available) to reduce the foreign assets to 20%, or just swap the excess RRSP assets for non-foreign ones outside your RRSP. In the last case, you get to retain ownership of everything—just rebalancing your portfolio to stay within the rules. (But be aware of the tax implications: cash will be subject to withholding tax and there is a potential for capital gains tax.)

What's foreign content?

Lots of things qualify, including mortgages held on foreign properties or lent to foreigners investing in Canada; limited partnerships (even if they are Canadian—because they already get favoured tax treatment); bonds issued by foreign governments (foreign-currency-pay bonds issued by Canadian governments are not considered foreign content); and stocks of non-Canadian companies, even if they trade on Canadian exchanges.

But for most people, foreign content comes in just one form: mutual funds.

One example is global bond funds, which invest in a basket of bonds from several countries. That reduces the risk to individual investors and counterbalances against inevitable currency fluctuations.

But there are those who argue eloquently against "wasting" your valuable foreign-content space on international bond funds. And it's an argument that makes sense: You can invest in the foreign-pay bonds of Canadian governments, Crowns and corporations (as well as a few other institutions, like the World Bank) to get the same protection against the falling dollar as the foreign bond funds, but without using any of your 20%. These bonds are all considered Canadian content, even though they pay you in other currencies.

> *So, this is probably the ultimate strategy: Use all*
> *your RRSP space for international equity funds—*
> *mutual funds that put their money into foreign*
> *stocks yielding you much higher long-term returns*
> *and more diversity of assets.*

There is no doubting the higher return most investors can get by going international. According to the Trust Company of the Bank of Montreal, over the last decade people who invested in Canadian mutual funds earned a total return of about 75%, whereas investors in global funds have enjoyed cumulative returns of up to 500%.

In fact the average compound rate of return of Canadian equity funds has been about 8%, while both American and international equity funds have yielded about 11%. In 1995, don't forget, the TSE 300 advanced by 16%, while the Dow Industrials in New York rocketed ahead more than 32%.

Meanwhile all those Canadians afraid of losing any of their money (most people) earned a glorious 6% in their long-term GICs, which, even sheltered from tax within an RRSP, were reduced last year by inflation to a real return of about 4.5%.

That's not investing. That's lunacy.

How to bend the 20% rule

There are a few legal ways to boost the effective foreign content in your RRSP past 20%. And you should employ some or all of these strategies.

- First, as mentioned already, get as much of an income stream in foreign currency as you want by investing in foreign-pay Canadian bonds. Major governments and government agencies issue bonds that will pay you interest in American dollars, Swiss francs or many other currencies.

   They are not considered foreign content and are completely eligible for your RRSP because Revenue Canada cares about the country issuing the bond, not the way it pays its bondholders. So, by loading up on these, you keep your valuable foreign-content room clear for the high-yielding international equity funds.

- There are several mutual funds that also do this—putting their money into foreign-pay Canadian bonds, making them RRSP-eligible but not being classified as foreign content.

- And speaking of mutual funds, you can also use Canadian funds to increase your foreign content. That's because many Canadian funds (including all Trimark funds) make sure they invest 20% of their cash in foreign assets. So, when you buy them, you are also upping your foreign exposure.

  For example, if you have $10,000 in your self-directed plan, you can put $2,000 into international equity funds as your foreign content. Then, if you bought $8,000 worth of units in Trimark, $1,600 of that (or 20%) would also be in foreign assets. That means your total foreign content would amount to $3,600 of your RRSP—or 36%. That's pretty close to double the amount allowed.

  Make sure you research the foreign-content level of any Canadian mutual fund you are considering buying. The higher it is, the more you will be protected against a declining Canadian dollar.

- You can also invest in international financial-institution bonds issued by outfits like the World Bank, which are denominated in American and other currencies. They are RRSP-eligible without having to use up your foreign-content room.

- And then, by holding the shares of a Canadian small business in your RRSP, you can jump your allowed foreign content up to 40%—double the regular limit. Ottawa will let you increase foreign content by three times the amount you have invested in that small business. The rules used to restrict small-business shares to 50% of the value of your RRSP, but now there is no limit.

HOW TO SPLIT INCOME WITH A SPOUSAL RRSP

Here's the typical drill for a lot of Canadian families: Dad works for four decades and ends up in the top tax bracket with a good pension or substantial RRSPs. Mom takes time out of the workforce to raise a family, has little retirement income and no personal savings. All of the family's liquid assets are in the hands of the man, who pays the most tax.

There is something wrong, and costly, with this picture. For example, a retired couple in B.C. living on one income of $70,000 will see $22,000 evaporate in taxes. But if that one income could be split into two, each at $35,000, the family tax savings would be almost $9,000, because they are both in a lower tax bracket.

If you need to be reminded how much $9,000 a year is, consider this: To earn that much money, after 40% tax, you'd have to have a five-year GIC yielding 6%, worth $250,000.

So, which is easier—finding an extra quarter-million dollars when you're retired, or making a few changes in your forties and fifties to shift assets into the hands of the less-taxed spouse? I thought so.

Revenue Canada does not allow you to just give money to your spouse. It has rules—called "attribution rules"—which attribute earned or investment income back to you in most cases. One of the best ways around this is to contribute to a spousal RRSP. This simply means putting money into a plan that your sweetie owns, and when he or she cashes the plan out, the money is taxed at your spouse's rate. If all works out well, that's a rate lower than yours.

Now before we talk about the mechanics of doing this, a special word of warning for everybody who is getting older: There is a growing bias in the Canadian tax system against seniors as Ottawa looks for money everywhere. The new Seniors Benefit, which will replace the OAS and GIS, clearly shows that. It will provide vastly less in benefits to Canadians because it will be calculated on family, not individual, income.

Then there is the clawback of the Pension Income credit and the Age Credit, which adds a significant tax burden on higher-income earners.

Consider what all this means:

> *A couple today with all the income and assets in the hands of one spouse is taxed at a high rate, while the proposed changes to the Seniors Benefit—basing benefits on family, not individual, income—would deny even the no-income spouse any government income.*

That may sound unfair, but get used to it. Just about all of today's middle-class Baby Boomers, Generation Xers and Echo Boomers will see no government cheques in retirement. Only the disabled and destitute will be cared for. The rest of us have to be smart as we prepare. And being smart means going spousal.

First, what's a spouse?

Of course, the government has a definition (after all, what are governments for?). A spouse is "a person of the opposite sex to whom the individual is married or with whom the individual has co-habited in a conjugal relationship for a period of at least one year, or less than one year if the two individuals are the natural or adoptive parents of a child."

If you are gay or lesbian, there's a good chance this definition might be changed in the near future, allowing your partner to be legally considered a spouse. Now that the current Parliament has amended the Charter of Rights and Freedoms to outlaw discrimination against sexual orientation, it seems only a matter of time.

For the rest of us, here's how it works today:

• Once you find out how much you can contribute to your RRSP this year, you have a choice: Put it all in your own plan, put it all in a plan in your spouse's name, or split it up between the two.

   In other words, you can put as much as you want into a spousal RRSP, so long as it does not exceed your personal annual-contribution limit.

• Of course, you can reduce your taxable income by the amount of the spousal RRSP contribution, just as with your own plan contributions.

• Your spousal contribution in no way affects your spouse's ability to contribute to his or her own plan, based on income. Just don't both of you contribute money to the same plan—the accounting is too complex when it comes to attributing for tax purposes. In fact, most banks and trusts won't even open up a joint RRSP for that reason.

• You can open a spousal plan any place where a normal RRSP is offered—banks, trust companies, credit unions, brokers, financial planning firms, etc. It does not cost extra.

• When you open the plan make it clear that it's for your spouse and, as with all of your RRSPs, ensure you put your spouse's name in as beneficiary.

• Money has to stay in the spousal plan for three years before it is considered his or hers. After that time, your spouse can take the money out at any time, and it will be taxed at his or her rate. Take it out before the three years are up, and it is attributed right back to you, and taxed in your hands.

• But here's a twist: If you are the higher-income earner and consider yourself a candidate for downsizing, outsourcing, restructuring or whatever other euphemism this wonderful decade comes up with, then the attribution rule can work in your favour.

If you are laid off, your spouse can withdraw money from his or her plan before three years have passed and it will be attributed back to you and taxed at your rate—which, when you are not employed, will be low.

- There is one circumstance under which spousal money can be taken out early with no attribution back to the contributor, and that's under the Home Buyers' Plan. Then you get to use it for a down-payment, and repay it within 15 years—no tax and no interest.

- Besides helping you to effectively split income in retirement, thereby shaving your taxes, a spousal RRSP can also help avoid the clawback on the existing Old Age Security and the Age Tax Credit.

   If your income is more than $53,000, the clawback is 15% of the amount above that, or your full OAS payment, whichever is less. So, by using a spousal RRSP, you can even out your two incomes and reduce the clawback. That means family income could be as high as $106,000 and both spouses would continue to receive the OAS.

   The same goes with the Age Credit, which is clawed back above an income of about $26,000. By splitting retirement income, a couple could earn $52,000, and both still get the credit.

   However, for anyone reading this book who is my age (47), or younger, you can pretty well forget about OAS, GIS, the Age Credit and the coming Seniors Benefit. These programs are luxuries that Canada will no longer be able to afford two decades from now, when a huge number of seniors overwhelms the government. But given what we know is coming, income-splitting seems even more important to avoid punitive levels of tax. Face it—seniors are easy to tax. Their income streams are usually from fixed-income investments or pensions. That makes them sitting ducks for governments desperate for more cash. You might as well split income, and make your duck as small as possible.

- Here's a good thing about a spousal RRSP: You can continue putting money into it, and getting a break on your own taxes, no matter what age you are, so long as your sweetie is 69 or younger.

   Yes, yes, another reason to rob the cradle.

- And when your spouse arrives at age 69, the spousal RRSP can be converted into a RRIF, just like any other plan. The money that has to be withdrawn under RRIF rules will be taxed at your spouse's rate. Any amount more than that will be attributed back to you, if you have made a spousal-plan contribution within the last three years.

Divorce, separation or marital breakdown

It happens. Frequently enough, in fact, that laws have been changed to deal quickly and decisively with retirement assets when the marriage or common-law relationship fails.

In this instance, a spousal RRSP is treated just the same as your own plan. And although the money you put in your spouse's plan over the years legally belongs to him or her, when separation or divorce occurs, all retirement assets are deemed to be the property of both spouses, no matter who put in what.

So, they are split fifty–fifty.

Given that, there is no reason not to contribute to a spousal plan. If the marriage does last into retirement, you split the income stream and reduce taxes. If it does not last, the assets are treated exactly the same way. Obviously, staying married is better.

As with just about any RRSP, your spousal plan should be self-directed, giving you maximum flexibility to swap assets that are right for the times. And remember that, once set up, those assets belong to the spouse, not to the contributor. Only he or she can take cash out, or authorize any activity within the plan.

YOUR RRSP AND YOUR REAL ESTATE

An RRSP can help you buy a home, under the existing rules. In fact, once you've got a house, you can even put your own mortgage inside your RRSP, and end up making mortgage payments to yourself.

> *Better still, working with a self-directed RRSP and the equity you've built up in your house, there is a way to actually transfer that equity into your tax-sheltered retirement plan—even if doing so means you exceed the allowed contribution levels.*

This is a bit tricky, and you need to follow the rules closely. In addition, this strategy works only if you already have an amount of cash (or cashable investments) in your RRSP equal to the current mortgage on your home or the one you plan to place on it, to get the equity out.

It is also going to cost you a few thousand dollars to set up, and a few hundred a year in fees. But if you feel like I do—that the future belongs to liquid assets, not to real assets like housing—then this is a dramatic way for you to turn your house into a retirement plan.

First, the mechanics of setting up an RRSP mortgage, and then the equity strategy.

How an RRSP mortgage works

Your RRSP is allowed to hold a mortgage on any Canadian real estate that you own—either residential or commercial—or on property owned by an immediate relative.

That means you can take money in your RRSP and lend it out as a mortgage. Then you must make regular payments back into your RRSP, just as you would with a bank mortgage.

One of the neat things about this is that you will end up paying far more back into your RRSP than you ever took out. **In fact, this is the only way you can contribute more to your RRSP than is allowed under the regular contribution rules.** Because of the way mortgages are amortized, payments in the early years are almost all interest. Only in the final years of a mortgage do you actually begin paying the principal back. So, over the course of a typical 25-year amortization, you will end up putting about three times more money into your RRSP than you took out.

In the meantime, you can use the payments made into your RRSP to invest in growth mutual funds, preferably based on the performance of international equities, to get solid double-digit returns.

> *So, the idea here is completely opposite to a conventional mortgage—which you want to pay off as fast as possible. The goal with an RRSP mortgage is to make it last as long as you can and be as costly as possible, so you can maximize the transfer of wealth into the retirement plan.*

There are several ways of doing this.

- First, go with the longest amortization period possible. The longer it takes you to pay it off, the more interest accrues and the greater the amount of money going into the RRSP.

- Second, the government stipulates that the rate of interest your RRSP mortgage is set at must be "comparable" to market rates. So shop around, finding the *highest possible rate* being offered commercially, and use that as your RRSP mortgage rate.

- Third, always make your RRSP mortgage an *open* one—which would allow you to pay it off at any time (which you have no intention of doing). Open mortgages cost a premium rate, which means your interest is greater.

  For example, as I write this, a one-year closed mortgage is at 6.5%, but by choosing the open option, that is boosted by three-quarters of a point, to 7.25%. That's a nice, high rate, considering that a one-year GIC is yielding just 4%.

- Fourth, you can make the mortgage a second one, to boost the interest rate even higher. (But this will also cost you more in mortgage insurance—all RRSP mortgages have to be insured by CMHC or GE Capital—the only two insurers currently available.)

- Finally, stay away from all the techniques that people normally use to accelerate repayment of the mortgages. In other words, you want a *monthly-pay* mortgage, instead of a weekly one that cuts repayment time and saves a lot in interest. You don't want to pay less into your RRSP, you want to pay as much as possible!

An RRSP mortgage has the same flexibility and the same constraints as a bank mortgage. You can choose any length of term commercially available, and if you default on your payments, your RRSP ends up taking ownership of your home—which you don't want.

That's because RRSPs are allowed to finance real estate, but not to own it. Your plan would be required to sell the home within a year, at market value.

There are certainly expensive set-up costs and moderate maintenance costs involved and, as mentioned, this has to be done through a self-directed retirement plan. But it's still worth it.

- To set the thing up will cost you an appraisal fee (typically $150 to $200), legal fees ($500 or more), and a one-time set-up fee (anywhere from $100 to $300, depending on the financial institution).

Also, all RRSP mortgages have to be insured, and the cost for that is generally about 2% of the mortgage amount, or $2,000 on a $100,000 loan. Normally, if you were smart, you'd pay this in cash rather than adding it to the mortgage principal, because by tacking it on, it also gets amortized and ends up costing you three times what you borrowed.

But in this instance, because the goal is to get money into your RRSP, you gladly add it to the outstanding debt.

- Once in place, the RRSP mortgage will have some ongoing costs. The annual fee for the self-directed plan is typically $150, and then there is a mortgage administration fee, which varies, from less than $100 to almost $300 annually. Revenue Canada stipulates that you can't administer your own RRSP mortgage—that needs to be done by a third-party agent, typically a trust company.

- Not all financial institutions will allow you to have an RRSP mortgage within a self-directed plan. Others will only allow such a mortgage on your principal residence. Still others are completely flexible—so shop around.

- As stated, you need to have enough cash or cashable assets in your RRSP to equal the mortgage you are transferring to your plan. If your RRSP assets are locked into GICs, for example, it won't work. And once the RRSP mortgage is set up, it's locked in until the time of renewal, when you have some options.

Using an RRSP mortgage to get equity out of your home

In most cases where people already have existing mortgages on their homes and less than $50,000 cash in their RRSP, it does not make sense to try to set up an RRSP mortgage. The initial and ongoing costs are too high to compete with the return your money could get elsewhere.

But there are some circumstances under which this strategy allows you to get equity out of real estate and at the same time exceed the RRSP contribution levels.

Is this you?

- You own your home, mortgage-free, which means you have a significant amount of equity (probably earning you 0%, because real-estate values almost everywhere in Canada are not exceeding the inflation rate);

- You have a whack of cash or cashable assets (Canada Savings Bonds, strip bonds, mutual funds, etc.) in your RRSP; and,

- You have a good cash flow, which you'd like to divert into your RRSP.

Here's the strategy for somebody with $150,000 equity in their home, and an equal amount in RRSP assets, invested in a 6% five-year GIC (the typical Canadian strategy).

1. Take out a home equity loan for $150,000. You can do this easily through financial institutions like ScotiaBank or Canada

Trust; or most full-service financial advisers will set it all up for you, sometimes even free of charge.

2. Invest that money in, say, equity-based mutual funds to earn at least 10%. Now your home-equity loan is deemed to be an investment loan for tax purposes.

3. As such, the interest on the equity loan is tax-deductible. So, if you are in the 54% tax bracket, when it comes time to do your income tax, deduct 54% of the interest you paid all year. Your taxable income will drop as a result, which is a nice extra.

4. Now, set up an RRSP mortgage, which means your retirement plan would buy out the bank or trust-company mortgage. You can insure this through GE Capital or, if you have waited up to a year after taking the equity loan, CMHC will insure the mortgage (CMHC has a rule against insuring equity loans, but after a period of time in existence it becomes a normal mortgage).

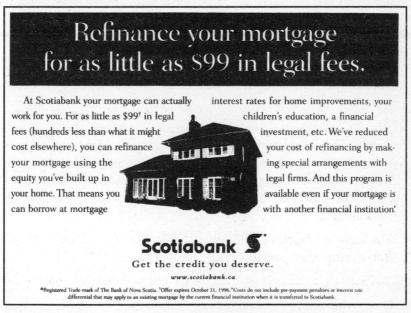

Scores of people are doing the smart thing: Cashing out the equity in their real estate and investing it in financial assets. Financial institutions like Scotiabank and Canada Trust have been leaders in home equity loans. Will they still be lending in five years if real estate continues to erode in value?

Source: Bank of Nova Scotia

Okay, let's review where we're at right now: You have taken $150,000 out of the equity in your home and it is now earning you at least 10% (instead of zero). At the same time, you have created a tax deduction, and reduced your income-tax load. And now your RRSP holds a $150,000 mortgage, instead of the assets that used to be there.

5. Now, every month, you cut a cheque to your RRSP in the form of a mortgage payment. At the current five-year rate of 8.5% (as I write this), that cheque would be for $1,207. And so, each year, you would be contributing $14,484 to your RRSP. Not only is that almost $1,000 more than the current maximum limit of $13,500, but it doesn't matter what your income level is. To make the maximum $13,500 payment, you'd have to be earning more than $75,000. But with an RRSP mortgage you could be contributing $14,484, in this case while making just $60,000—which would normally qualify you for a maximum contribution of only $10,800.

6. In five years, you would be able to contribute $72,470 into your RRSP and, of course, during that time, if all the money were put into growth-oriented mutual funds averaging 10% (and you should do much better than that), your RRSP would have about $93,000 returned to it.

The bottom line is increased wealth. Five years after having $150,000 equity in your home and $150,000 in your RRSP (which had grown to just over $200,000), for a total of $350,000, you would have a $150,000 mortgage in your RRSP, $93,000 in new RRSP assets and over $200,000 in outside investments (assuming the $150,000 grew by about 12% after capital gains tax)—for a total of almost $450,000.

If you had not arranged the equity loan and then the RRSP mortgage, the $150,000 in your RRSP would certainly have continued to grow, but the equity in your home likely would not have grown, and might even have shrunk. And you would not have had the mortgage interest to help reduce your taxable income.

With such things possible, isn't it amazing most people continue to sit on all that money in their homes?

The Home Buyers' Plan

RRSP mortgages are a great way for people with equity to get money out and to increase their RRSP contributions. The Home Buyers' Plan is geared, in contrast, to first-time buyers—and it is mired in controversy. As an MP, I lobbied for this plan to come into effect, and let me tell you why.

It was in 1991, during the depths of the recession, with real-estate activity low and the economy hurting badly. The residential-construction sector had suffered terribly, with substantial job losses, and the Canadian Real Estate Association came up with the idea of letting people temporarily borrow money from their RRSPs to buy a home.

I told CREA I would help and, along with other supportive MPs, we convinced Finance Minister Don Mazankowski to give it a shot. He did in the 1992 budget, and the response was unreal—within a year almost a quarter-million people borrowed more than $2 billion to finance houses, and by the spring of 1993, the economy was looking a lot better.

Originally the program was to end in early 1994, but the current Finance minister, Paul Martin, surprised a lot of people by making it permanent.

And now I have second thoughts.

The plan did what it was intended to do—give a shot of adrenaline to the housing market when it was really needed. At the time, those against it argued that the measure corrupted the whole intent of the RRSP system, which was clearly to encourage people to put money away for retirement, not for buying a house.

Although I realize the Home Buyers' Plan is still popular, and supported by the real-estate industry, the critics' arguments got a lot stronger and more valid when the plan was carved in stone. And, yes, there are dangers inherent in using this plan, unless you know how to work it and what to do once the plan is in effect.

I'll get to those points in a moment.

Here's how it works

You are allowed to withdraw up to $20,000 from existing funds in your RRSP to buy a home. If you have a spouse, together you can withdraw up to $40,000. At first, the plan was open to anyone, but now it has been restricted to first-time buyers.

So you are eligible if you are a Canadian resident with an RRSP who has not used this plan before and have not owned a home in the last five years, or are married to or living with someone (of the opposite sex) who has not owned for five years.

The money you withdraw has to be used to buy an existing or to-be-built house by October 1 of the year following the withdrawal. It can be a condo, detached home, mobile trailer, apartment unit in a duplex or triplex, co-operative or townhouse. But the money can't be used to pay down an existing mortgage or fix up a house you already own. To apply, simply fill out the right form (Home Buyers' Plan—Withdrawal Application, which your bank or trust should have on file) and then you can withdraw the money from your RRSP and no taxes will be withheld.

You are, in effect, taking an interest-free loan from your own RRSP, which you will have to pay back. If you miss a repayment, then it becomes part of your income that year, which means you pay tax on it, and lose the ability to put it back into your RRSP bubble.

How the interest-free loan is repaid

You must put the money back into your RRSP within 15 years of taking it out—in equal payments. So the maximum $20,000 interest-free and tax-free loans would have to be repaid in annual instalments of $1,333. Miss one, and $1,333 will be added to your income, costing you more tax.

The repayments start in the second calendar year after you borrow, giving new home buyers a while to get their financial house in order. So, a loan taken in 1997 under the Home Buyers' Plan will need repayments beginning in 1999.

But even that can be delayed.

The rules for repayment were changed to the same timetable as RRSP contributions—which is 60 days into the next year. So, borrow in 1997 and you don't have to make the first payment until March 1, 2000.

There is no rule saying the repayments have to be made into the same RRSP they came out of, but, of course, you can't claim a tax deduction when you make a repayment—you already got that when the money first went in. So, make sure the bank, trust company, broker or whoever has your plan is aware, and fill out the RRSP repayment form.

Revenue Canada has just started sending out borrowers' notification forms giving an annual statement—watch for it, and it will tell you exactly how much is due, and by when. It also includes a summary of the payments you've already made. You can always pay back more than you are required to, but not less. And when you do make an overpayment, future payments will be scaled back to reflect that.

If you are turning 69 and your plan isn't paid back, you can pay it out in full if you have the money, or include it in your income each year, and spread the tax liability out.

A neat strategy to use

The rules are clear: You can make an RRSP contribution and take out a tax-free, interest-free loan under the Home Buyers' Plan in the same year. The two actions just have to be at least 90 days apart.

Here's what that can mean: If you are planning to buy a home, and you don't have an RRSP, you can make the closing date on the real-estate transaction 90 days or more from the time of signing the offer.

Then go to the bank, trust or personal adviser and open an RRSP, putting in $20,000 (if you have the accumulated room). That will earn you a tax-rebate cheque from the government of $8,000 if you're in the 40% tax bracket.

Then, on closing, use the Home Buyers' Plan to withdraw the $20,000, without penalty. Now you have just increased your wealth by $8,000 in three months, for a few minutes' work filling out two forms. For first-time home buyers, $8,000 extra can sure come in handy down the road for appliances, decorating, furniture—or (better still) reducing the mortgage principal.

But the plan can also be dangerous

As I said above, the point of RRSPs is to encourage people to save for their retirement. With an aging population and a bankrupt government, this is certainly something you want to do.

The Home Buyers' Plan was intended to be a temporary stimulus to a sick and dying real-estate industry, and it worked. But since it has become permanent, it represents a serious precedent for using the $150-billion pot of RRSP funds for things that have nothing to do with retirement. If we allow people to finance real estate with their RRSPs, then why shouldn't entrepreneurs be able to finance their business ventures the same way?

Those questions are now being asked, and any threat to our RRSP system is deadly serious.

But here is the greater concern for somebody taking money out of their RRSP to buy a home: There is no way the value of that house is going to grow enough in the next three decades to compensate for the lost power of that $20,000 (or whatever the amount borrowed) growing tax-free within your retirement plan. And the younger you are, the more money you will lose. Ironically, the bulk of the people using the Home Buyers' Plan are younger, first-time buyers—the people for whom this plan is the most dangerous.

In fact, that $20,000 taken out of an RRSP in your twenties can be worth a lost $200,000 when you are in your sixties. Will your real estate rise ten times in value between now and the year 2037? I seriously doubt it. If it paces inflation, you'll be doing well.

So, think hard and long before you simply remove the money for a down-payment. And if you decide to borrow, pay it back into your plan as fast as possible—not spreading it out over a long decade and a half. And certainly keep putting money into an RRSP after you buy the house. Get on a monthly contribution plan. Like a regular car-loan payment, after a few months, you won't even notice it coming out of your account—but what a difference it will make when you retire in that house with a few mill in the bank!

Just think of your monthly RRSP contributions as a payback on the money you saved reducing the mortgage by the amount of your Home Buyers' Plan loan.

BUILDING YOUR RRSP WITHOUT ANY CASH

Revenue Canada will pay you money to shelter assets you already own from tax. Honest. Here's why, and how.

Any financial security that qualifies to be in an RRSP can be put into a plan at any time, instead of cash. You can use assets you already own to make your annual contribution (up to your yearly limit), or you can transfer assets into your plan to use up the carry-forward on unused past contributions.

In return for doing that, the government will send you money— because the contribution of assets you already own will be treated the same way as a cash contribution. In other words, you will still get the tax deduction or refund.

This is called a "contribution in kind" by Revenue Canada. But I call it the excuse-breaker. With this rule in place, there is no excuse for just about anybody to miss an RRSP contribution, because almost all of us own something, at some time, that could be dumped in the tax shelter.

Let me give you the example of another woman I work with who came to me with a simple question: Should she borrow money to make an RRSP contribution?

Sure, I said, that makes sense. But maybe there's an even better strategy. And I asked her what assets she already had. It turned out she had $7,000 in Canada Savings Bonds, purchased in the fall of 1995, paying 5.25%.

Because these bonds were not in an RRSP, and because she was in the 41% tax bracket, the after-tax return was actually closer to 3%. And, after inflation of 1.5%, the real return was pathetic—it was almost not worth having the investment at all. So, we used the "contribution in kind" rule and a couple of other techniques to turn the $7,000 into $39,000 and give her double-digit rates of return.

- First, she called her financial adviser and opened a self-directed RRSP. That cost just over $100.

- Then she transferred the CSBs into the plan, at a value of slightly more than $7,000, because of accrued interest. And she cashed them in.

- Now she went to the bank and got an RRSP loan, at prime, for $2,800, and contributed that money to her plan, reaching her personal contribution level of just under $10,000. The bank waived repayment until she got her tax refund (of $2,870) for making the contribution in kind to her RRSP. And she used the refund to repay the loan.

- So, now she had about $10,000 in her self-directed RRSP, and was already way ahead of the game—more assets with the ability to grow free of tax.

Then we used the money to buy a Province of Ontario strip bond maturing in 2010, with a maturity value of $39,000. She can hold the bond until then, and get all that money, or she can sell it at any time, if interest rates drop, and get a capital gain as the price of the bond rises. Either way, she wins.

The benefits here are obvious—a dramatic increase in assets and an investment with a good rate of return, shielded from tax.

As I hope you can see, money can be grown, without risk of any kind, using today's generous and flexible RRSP rules and a little investment common sense. But too many people don't understand the basics, thinking an RRSP is not for them while they sit on taxable investments that could—with one phone call—be both free of tax and leveraged much higher in value.

It's time you examined your own portfolio. Yes, right now. Write down all the assets you own. If any of them qualifies to go into a self-directed RRSP, and you have not made this year's contribution, or have unused contribution room from previous years, then call your financial adviser and make a contribution in kind.

CONTRIBUTIONS IN KIND

Qualifying securities	Yes, I own	Value
Canada Savings Bonds	_____	_____
Corporate bonds	_____	_____
Government bonds	_____	_____
GICs	_____	_____
Mutual-fund units	_____	_____
Limited-partnership units	_____	_____
Provincial savings bonds	_____	_____
Mortgages	_____	_____
Small-business shares	_____	_____
Stocks	_____	_____
Term deposits	_____	_____
Strip bonds	_____	_____
Treasury bills	_____	_____
Cash	_____	_____
Cashable GICs	_____	_____

As you can see, there are many securities that can be put in your RRSP in lieu of cash. Consider how much better off a middle-aged couple would be in retirement if every year they took a chunk of their portfolio and tax-sheltered it by making a contribution in kind, especially right into a spousal RRSP if one is in a lower tax bracket. Instead of ending up with fully taxable investments in the hands of the one paying the most to Revenue Canada, they would drastically improve their financial security.

Here are some rules to remember:

• You have to start with a self-directed RRSP. And don't let this scare you—you don't need to administer it yourself, that's the job of your financial adviser, whether it's your own planner or someone at the bank. It will cost you $100 or so a year, which is money well spent.

In fact, all you really need for RRSP planning is one self-administered plan, because within it you can hold whatever you want. Never get talked into some low-paying GIC RRSP when you go to make an RRSP contribution.

• You can't make a contribution in kind larger than your annual RRSP limit plus any carry-forward room from previous years.

- The asset you do contribute in kind has to be properly valued. If it's mutual-fund units, then the market value on the day of transfer is the value, not the price you first paid for them. If it's a strip bond, the same applies (a bond gets more valuable as it nears maturity). Canada Savings Bonds are credited to your RRSP for both the face value and compound interest.

- Revenue Canada rules stipulate that when the asset is transferred into your RRSP, it's the same as if it was sold. So if it has risen in value, you may have a tax liability. In the case of a stock or mutual fund, for example, that could generate a capital gain, which you must include in your taxable income for the year.

- If, however, the asset has declined in value since you bought it, don't transfer it directly into your self-administered RRSP. Why? Because you will not be able to claim a capital loss if you do that. Instead, sell the security and then use the cash to make the RRSP contribution. Now you can claim that capital loss against any capital gains you might have.

- The rules also allow you to substitute assets you currently have inside your self-directed RRSP for assets you own on the outside— so long as they are qualifying assets. For example, if you needed cash and didn't want to borrow it from the bank, you could borrow it from your RRSP.

  That means, you could transfer mutual-fund units held outside the plan for assets inside that could be converted to cash (Canada Savings Bonds, for example). So, you get the cash you need without having had to sell the funds—triggering a capital gain.

- You can use the substitution rule as well to fine-tune your RRSP, making sure you have the proper things inside it. For example, if you have any investments that pay you interest (GICs, for example) or that do not give you annual income but on which you still need to pay annual tax (like strip bonds), then they should be the first things stuck inside the RRSP. That will provide you the greatest tax relief.

  Other investments, like stocks that pay you dividends, should be on the outside. That's because inside the RRSP you can't use the dividend tax credit, which saves tax.

  Substituting an asset for another one doesn't affect your annual contribution limit and it doesn't earn you a tax rebate. There is no restriction on how often you want to swap assets, but some institutions will charge you a fee.

- Do these things now. There is absolutely no guarantee that the "contribution in kind" rule won't be quashed in the next budget. And, as mentioned earlier, there is also no guarantee your ability to carry forward missed contributions won't be curtailed, or even eliminated. While it is so simple—just one phone call—to tax-shelter assets you already own, earning a tax rebate and substantially increasing your rate of return, why the heck wouldn't you do it?

Moving tax-sheltered money

It's possible to move money between different RRSPs that you own, from an RRSP to a RRIF (registered retirement income fund) or vice versa, or from a pension plan to or from an RRSP. The rules are reasonable, but also complicated, and you should certainly get professional advice before doing so.

- If you have various plans at several institutions, you should transfer them to one self-directed plan. That will give you the most options and flexibility. The transfer won't affect your annual-contribution limit or get you a tax refund. And you don't need to include it on your income-tax return.

  But you do need to fill out the proper paperwork. Your financial adviser, or the institution to which the transfer is being made, will handle that for you. And sometimes the place from which your transfer is coming will give you grief—imposing fees or penalties or delaying the move. I have even come across cases when money earmarked for a transfer out has been lost!

- Money can move tax-free between an RRSP and a RRIF under certain circumstances. If you take too much money out of a RRIF, for example, you can transfer the excess back into an RRSP, if you are under 70 and have the contribution room. Or, RRSP money can be used to set up a RRIF at any time. Of course, the only place that RRIF money can come from is an RRSP, an annuity or another RRIF. More on retirement income funds later.

- A lump sum of money can be transferred from a registered pension plan into an RRSP, but it has to be done directly. You can't get the pension money and then put it in your RRSP without being dinged for tax along the way.

- The same holds true for transfers from retirement or severance packages. The money must be put directly into your RRSP. Remember: If you take a cheque, you'll lose up to 30% in taxes right off the top.

- And there are only a couple of instances when money can be transferred from your own RRSP into somebody else's—when your marriage goes bust, or you die, both of which can be unsettling emotionally and financially.

In the instance of marital breakdown, the law requires that retirement assets be split evenly. That means RRSP money can be transferred directly into your ex-spouse's plan (or RRIF). For this to happen, you have to be living apart, and your significant other has to have met the definition of "spouse"—the opposite sex, married or common-law, or with whom you've had a child.

If you get back together again, the retirement assets may revert to your spouse's plan—which is an interesting form of income-splitting. (There's nothing about this in the Income Tax Act, and Revenue Canada admits it's a grey area. But lawyers will try anything on for size.)

As for death, Revenue Canada considers this the equivalent of cashing in your RRSP or RRIF, and your estate has to pay tax on the whole amount. This is a good argument for spending all your money before you die.

But if you want to leave money for others, there are a couple of ways. Easiest is simply making sure all your retirement plans designate your spouse as beneficiary. After death, the assets will simply and quickly flow to him or her. It's worth checking now that you have done this in the proper place on your RRSP documents.

If your spouse has an RRSP, the money goes there free of tax. If he or she does not have an RRSP (and you don't want this to be the case), then the money is taxable.

And if there is no spouse, a child or grandchild may be designated, but only if nobody else has claimed a tax credit for that child, if the kid's income is under $6,456, or if he or she is physically or mentally disabled. In these cases, the assets can flow into an RRSP tax-free. Also, a dependant child under 18 can get funds tax-free to purchase an annuity.

Otherwise, the money can be used to purchase an annuity for the child, through a formula based on his or her age. This is an integral part of estate planning, and the best advice I can give is this: Long before you face the end, make sure you plan the disposition of your estate, working with a professional.

CARRYING FORWARD YOUR UNUSED CONTRIBUTIONS

As mentioned earlier, the rules were changed in the last federal budget allowing you to unconditionally carry forward RRSP contributions that you should have made but, for some reason, did not. Prior to March 1996, you were limited to seven years for carry-forward. Now there is no limit (although I'll argue later that a new limit is probably not far off).

This may sound like having your cake and eating it too. And, in some ways, using your money now to pay down the mortgage, secure in the knowledge you can catch up on retirement savings later, is comforting. In other ways, not making your full RRSP contribution every year is a very bad idea. The unlimited carry-forward provision may end up hurting a lot of Canadians.

Already we are vastly behind in our savings contributions. In 1994, for example, we put into our RRSPs only 16.6% of what the rules allowed. That was down a few points from the Nineties average of about 20%.

Why are we leaving 80% or more of the allowable contribution (and huge tax savings) sitting on the table each year? There are several reasons:

- Following the 1990s recession, family finances are just too strung-out to allow "extra" cash for a retirement contribution.

- Canadians are generally unaware that, given cheap interest rates and rising financial markets, it makes perfect sense to borrow for the annual RRSP contribution.

- Not enough people are doing it the easy way—making monthly contributions through preapproved bank plans or payroll deductions.

- General ignorance of the fact that you can make a contribution in kind, just putting existing assets in an RRSP—no cash—and still getting a tax refund.

- The carry-forward rule gives a false sense of security by taking away the urgency to contribute regularly, every 12 months.

    Whatever the reason, this has helped create a very serious situation, when we are meeting only 20% or less of the goal. And that's exactly what the annual-contribution limit is—the goal.

Too few Canadians realize that the RRSP limits do not come out of a hat. They have been carefully created by actuaries to meet assumptions about demographics, income needs, future economic conditions and public pensions.

> *The RRSP contribution limit is the recommended amount you should be putting away every year, without significantly altering your lifestyle. The assumption is you will contribute for 35 years. So, if you're over 30 and don't have an RRSP, you're behind.*

Many people are massively behind—well into their forties and early fifties with little, or nothing, saved. Together, we have more than $110 billion in catching-up to do—the amount of carry-forward that has accumulated. In fact, the unused contributions from previous years now account for over 70% of the total amount we can contribute this year.

Some people think fortysomething Baby Boomers, just entering their peak career and earning years, will make up a lot of lost ground in the next couple of years. Others point to sizeable inheritances Boomers will receive as their parents pass on.

But I think both points are overstated. Middle-aged Baby Boomers are, on average, way behind with their retirement savings, having socked away little more than $30,000 on average, in Canada—enough to finance less than a year in retirement. Many of them simply will never be able to make up that lost ground. And as for inheritances, they are currently being spent by the longest-living and healthiest senior generation in North American history. In fact, many Boomers will be hitting retirement with their parents still alive.

So, there is no easy or fast solution to the problem of the coming retirement crisis. Today's Baby Boomers should make use of their carry-forward immediately, and then get on a regular schedule of RRSP contributions, ideally monthly and by automatic withdrawal.

Here are some other strategies regarding the carry-forward provision:

- Younger taxpayers could concentrate on raising a family or paying down real estate, saving up unused RRSP contributions until they are in a higher tax bracket, and so earning a bigger refund.

  The danger here is that you don't get into the habit of making RRSP contributions; you are not building up savings that can compound, tax-free, for that extra period of time; and there is no guarantee the government won't close the door on the ability to carry forward unused room.

- There's also the danger of building up carry-forward that you will never be able to use. It doesn't take many years of missed contributions to amass a great deal of unused deduction room.

- If you do gain an inheritance, be careful about how you use your carry-forward allowance. Dumping a great deal of money into an RRSP could temporarily drop you into a lower tax bracket, meaning a lesser refund. Or, it could make you subject to the alternative minimum tax, which was introduced in 1986 to make sure wealthy people could not use deductions to reduce their taxable income to zero.

- Not making a regular annual contribution means losing the use of annual tax refunds. Remember, if you are in the 40% tax bracket, a $10,000 contribution earns you a $4,000 cheque from Ottawa—money that can be reinvested in your retirement plan (using the carry-forward), or used to pay down the RRSP loan.

- But the most damaging aspect of postponing your RRSP contribution is the lost earnings that result from the tax-free compounding of assets. Missing just one $5,000 contribution when you're forty can result in a loss of retirement income more than three times higher.

So, here's the bottom line:

> **The carry-forward provision is a gift for those who have just discovered they are behind, and are allowed to catch up. Make sure you do catch up, and as quickly as possible. Borrow to do this, or use contributions in kind, putting the tax refund into your plan.**

For those people who don't make a full contribution this year, figuring they will catch up later, be very aware of the danger in this strategy.

- The ability to carry forward unused contributions could end at any time.

- The addition of each unused contribution just makes it that much harder to ever get all that money into your plan.

- You are losing out on the greatest power of the RRSP—to allow assets to compound in value, tax-free, over a long period of time.

- You are forgoing annual tax-rebate cheques that can increase your wealth.

- You're gambling you will be in a higher tax bracket later, when just the opposite could be the case.

- And you are clearly falling behind. The annual contribution you can make is the one you should make—year after year for at least 35 years.

Putting off your RRSP contributions is like saying you're going to take off 20 pounds next year. Has anyone in history ever done that?

I rest my case.

SHOULD YOU MAKE AN OVERCONTRIBUTION?

The law cuts you some slack by allowing your RRSP to have more money in it than the rules normally allow. It used to be a sizeable whack of money—up to $8,000 in a cumulative lifetime overcontribution.

This was a gift, because while the $8,000 did not give you a tax refund when it went in, it still sat there and earned tax-free returns year after year. So, lots of smart people made sure they carried an overcontribution of that amount in their plans, or their spousal RRSP.

The speculation before the 1995 budget was that the $8,000 would be reduced or eliminated as Paul Martin started to tighten up on RRSPs—and it was right. Ottawa chopped the $8,000 right down to $2,000 and, in so doing, caused lots of people who had taken the higher amount to make adjustments to their plans.

The penalty for having more than the allowed amount of money in your RRSP is a charge of 1% a month on the excess contribution, until you get rid of it. The penalty must be paid within three months of the end of the year in which you had the excess in your plan. Miss that deadline and Revenue Canada will also hit you with arrears.

Effective budget day 1995 (February 26), when the allowed overcontribution dropped to $2,000, taxpayers with more in their plans were given some time to come onside.

Let's say you had $8,000 in overcontribution to your plan on budget day two years ago. That means you are $6,000 over the new limit. No penalty will be assessed, but you can't make a new RRSP contribution —ever—until that $6,000 is used up.

So, the next year, the first $6,000 of the amount you can contribute is taken up by the money already in your plan. If you were eligible to contribute $8,000 to your RRSP, that would work out to be $6,000 in existing overcontribution, and just $2,000 in new money.

But the good news is you get a tax refund based on your full contribution limit of $8,000.

There is no time limit for getting your overcontribution down to $2,000, but obviously it's in your interest to do it quickly so that you: (a) get the tax refund and get it working for you; and (b) resume your regular contributions.

Does it make sense to overcontribute to your RRSP?

The most obvious answer is yes: Whenever you are given the opportunity of moving more capital into your tax shelter, you should do so, even when making that overcontribution does not give you a tax refund. It is astonishing how fast money can grow when it is shielded from taxes.

> *If you're my age (47) and you overcontribute $2,000 and manage to average 10% a year (not difficult with conservative, equity-based mutual funds), when you're 67 it will have grown into $13,000. If you are fortunate enough to be 27 years old, and overcontribute the same amount at the same rate of return, when you're 67 it will have turned into more than $90,000!*

That's the power of tax-free compounding, and this clearly shows the advantage of stuffing your RRSP at every opportunity.

You can have an overcontribution of $2,000 living inside your plan for decades—and then use it as part of an annual contribution, getting a tax refund. So, who is ideally suited to use an overcontribution strategy?

• Obviously, young people. The younger the better, starting at 19, which is the minimum age for carrying an overcontribution. It makes sense for parents to make an overcontribution in the name of a child who does not have earned income and can't contribute to his or her own plan.

You won't get a tax deduction, but by the time that child reaches the age of 59, he or she will be wealthier by about $90,000, thanks to your $2,000 gift.

• Retired people who still have earned income (like rental income) can overcontribute, and then get the tax deduction back, even if your RRSP has been converted into a RRIF. So long as you continue to have that income, claim the deduction yearly at the rate of 18% of what you are earning—until the full $2,000 is used up.

The same thing goes for spousal RRSPs, so long as your spouse is 69 or younger. You can make an overcontribution, and then get the money back in deductions from your earned income.

• However, if you make the overcontribution before you retire, and don't have earned income, the money will be taxed twice: first, because you didn't get a refund when it went into the plan (it was already in after-tax dollars), and, second, because, when it comes out of your RRIF as income, it's taxed again.

There may be a way of getting that money back, but it's complicated. You must show that you reasonably expected to have earned income to qualify you for a deduction—and that something went wrong. You also have to convince Revenue Canada you didn't make the overcontribution just to get it into your plan with the idea you'd get it back later through a deduction (which, of course, you did). Good luck.

• Another reason to carry an overcontribution is to give a little personal protection in case you are unexpectedly laid off or incapacitated.

Next year you might qualify to make an RRSP contribution (based on this year's earnings), but if you're out of work, it's unlikely you'd have the money. In that case, claim the $2,000 overcontribution that you've been carrying as your RRSP contribution. That will earn you a refund cheque, just at a time you could use it.

Making an overcontribution makes perfect sense so long as you're careful to avoid going over the $2,000 limit. The real purpose is to get as much money as possible into your plan for the longest possible period of time, at the highest rate of return.

So, if you do make an overcontribution, don't be content to have it sitting around growing at 5 or 6% in a GIC. Go for a growth mutual fund with the potential of doubling your money twice every decade.

THE CANADIAN MISTAKE: BEING TOO CONSERVATIVE

Every year Canadians contribute just a fraction of what they could to their RRSPs, for reasons already discussed. What a tragedy. But, compounding the mistake, most of those who do contribute end up wimping out because they are afraid of taking a risk. They end up investing tax-sheltered retirement funds in GICs or savings bonds. Both, in my view, are a disaster and likely to remain so for the next decade.

Here's what I believe:

• The North American economy will grow strongly, thanks to demographics.

• Inflation will be no real threat.

• Central banks want lower interest rates.

• GICs taken out today at low rates will probably come up for renewal at even lower rates. Meanwhile, cheap money will fuel stock values.

• An aging Baby Boom generation will soon gorge itself on mutual funds, government bonds and equities to get the double-digit returns it so badly needs.

• This will accelerate the shift from real assets (like your house) to financial assets.

• Stock markets will continue to climb, albeit with corrections along the way. But, over time, there is no real risk in the market.

• We are all living extraordinarily long lives. If you are in your thirties or forties today, you could have 30 years in retirement to finance.

• Government pensions are an endangered species. Don't count on one.

If you share these beliefs, then it's obvious the greatest threat we all face is outliving the pool of money we are amassing for decades in retirement. The risk is not losing money; it's not growing enough.

But not enough Canadians realize that yet, so they continue to invest their RRSP money in the wrong places, and they have the wrong asset mix.

Asset allocation

Investing in your RRSP is important. Where your RRSP invests is even more important. You have three basic choices, or classes of assets. Each has a different level of risk and return associated to it:

Source: *The Toronto Sun*

Cash equivalents
Low risk and low return. These are liquid investments that can be converted to cash quickly and on which it is impossible to actually lose money. Included are Canada Savings Bonds, provincial savings bonds, short-term bank deposits, T-bill and money-market mutual funds.

Fixed-income
Low to medium risk, low to moderate return. These pay you regular income at a fixed rate, but vary quite a bit in their flexibility. The main three contenders are GICs, bond or mortgage funds and government bonds (not savings bonds).

- *Guaranteed Investment Certificates (GICs).* These are what most people opt for because they spell out how much money you will have upon maturity and they are insured against loss up to $60,000. But there are some serious drawbacks: Interest rates are low and probably going lower; the money is locked up for years; and there's no potential for a capital gain. I wouldn't put a nickel of RRSP money in a GIC.

- *Bond and Mortgage Funds.* Mutual funds that invest in pools of government bonds or residential mortgages. They are attractive to people who want low risk and a predictable yield. But many investors do not realize these funds are a terrible place to have money: when interest rates rise, they drop in value. That happened a couple of years ago and thousands got burned.

% HOLDING MUTUAL FUNDS BY FUND TYPE

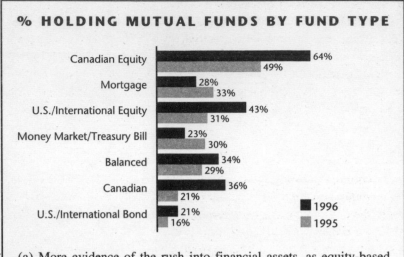

(a) More evidence of the rush into financial assets, as equity-based mutual fund holdings mushroomed last year. Meanwhile, falling rates have investors deserting money market funds.

Source: Deloitte and Touche

WHY PEOPLE DO NOT INVEST IN MUTUAL FUNDS

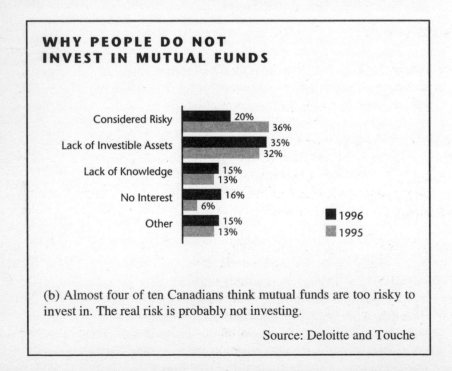

(b) Almost four of ten Canadians think mutual funds are too risky to invest in. The real risk is probably not investing.

Source: Deloitte and Touche

- *Government Bonds.* A much better choice. You can buy regular government bonds that pay you interest on a periodic basis. Or (my favourite), strip bonds—bonds that have had the interest stripped from them, so they pay no income but are bought at a big discount to face value. The advantages over a GIC are extreme: better rate of interest, cashable anytime, yield a capital gain if interest rates fall, and 100% government guaranteed. See "Wealth without risk: Strip bonds" in Chapter 5.

Growth assets

Higher risk, much higher return. These are the assets that earn you capital gains and that appreciate much faster—but that are also vulnerable to short-term declines, sometimes extreme. They are best for the buy-and-hold investor who realizes building RRSP assets is a long-term project. The two you should concentrate on are equities and mutual funds.

- *Equities.* Also known as stocks. You take up an equity, or ownership, position in a company when you invest in its stock, or shares. These shares are traded in a variety of ways and places, and constantly change in value according to the economy, the company's performance and the laws of supply and demand. Although the stock market has marched steadily higher over the last 100 years, not all stocks have gained, and there have been severe corrections lasting years and stripping wealth from stockholders. Risk varies greatly—invest in bank stocks and receive steady, moderate growth, or pick a junior resource stock and get rich or destitute in a few months.

- *Mutual Funds.* These are pools of assets managed by professionals. Instead of trying to pick your own stocks, for example, you buy units in a fund that invests in dozens, or hundreds, of stocks. Funds can invest in all kinds of things, and there are well over 1,000 to choose from. It might seem like an impossible task to pick four or six, which is why that's best left to your adviser. The important thing is to concentrate on long-term growth.

> **The farther you are from retirement, the more money you should have in growth assets.**

If you are in your twenties or thirties, there is nothing wrong with putting 100% of your retirement savings into high-octane, equity-based mutual funds. In your forties and fifties, being 50% into equity funds

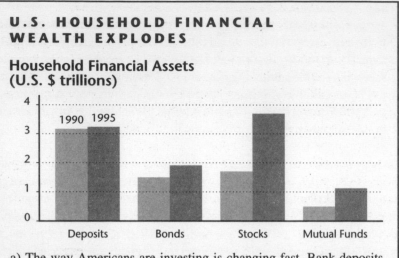

U.S. HOUSEHOLD FINANCIAL WEALTH EXPLODES

Household Financial Assets (U.S. $ trillions)

a) The way Americans are investing is changing fast. Bank deposits are about the same; money into bonds is up a quarter; while investments in stocks and mutual funds have doubled.

Source: Nesbitt Burns

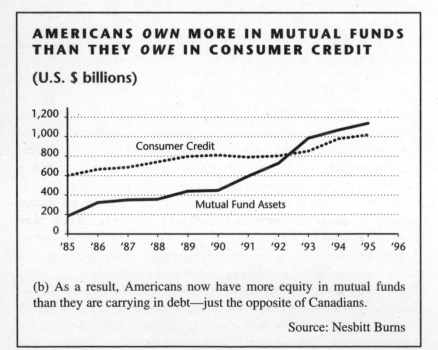

AMERICANS *OWN* MORE IN MUTUAL FUNDS THAN THEY *OWE* IN CONSUMER CREDIT

(U.S. $ billions)

(b) As a result, Americans now have more equity in mutual funds than they are carrying in debt—just the opposite of Canadians.

Source: Nesbitt Burns

with the rest in fixed income is still a conservative strategy.

And senior investors also need growth. The prevailing wisdom that seniors should invest only in fixed-income, especially GICs, is simply wrong. Anybody under the age of 80 should have growth assets.

For the essential ten rules of successful mutual-fund investing, see the updated 1997 version of my book *2015: After the Boom*. Any middle-aged person serious about financing his or her retirement has no option but to invest in mutual funds—immediately, and often.

And stop being Canadian, eh?

American families with mutual-fund investments have, on average, $97,000 there. Canadian families with mutual funds have an average of just $42,000. The Americans are twice as invested in funds as we are and, in my view, will build their wealth twice as quickly. In fact, it's already happening.

Just look at the way Americans are changing their investment habits. In the period from 1990 to 1995, U.S. families upped their bond investments by a quarter, and doubled the money they are pumping into stocks and mutual funds. As a result, U.S. household financial wealth is exploding, while a record number of Canadians are declaring bankruptcy. And now Americans own more in mutual-fund assets—for the first time ever—than they owe in consumer credit. Meanwhile Canadian household debt is at an all-time high.

We may be great savers, but we are only just starting to learn about investing. And we'd better learn fast.

RRSPs, THE SEQUEL: CONVERTING TO A RRIF

Okay, now you have been a good little Canadian, used all the neat RRSP strategies, saved like a crazed beaver and have built up a retirement nest egg. You are approaching age 69. What comes next?

The rules say this is the end of your RRSP. You are no longer allowed to make contributions and use those to reduce your taxes. Now you have to start taking money out—and that can be done in one of three ways.

Take cash and your tax hit now

Option one is to simply cash in all or part of your RRSPs by collapsing the plans. The down-side is you'll be hit for income taxes when this happens—up to 30% will be withheld at source.

So, why would anyone do this?

Actually, prior to the 1996 federal budget, it made just about no sense to cash out RRSPs in early retirement, but the situation has changed, as mentioned earlier, because of the proposed Seniors Benefit.

Remember that, starting in 2001, the feds plan to replace the OAS and GIS with a guaranteed-income scheme that will result in double taxation on most retirement income. Middle-class seniors can expect to fork over at least 50% of their income in tax after the change. So, reasonable tax planning means you should reduce your income stream and get your wealth working in other ways prior to reaching age 65.

This means people who are 60 or younger today should get immediate advice from a financial adviser and then start restructuring their affairs. I am sure for many, many people part of that restructuring will involve collapsing RRSPs prior to the retirement age.

Doing so will clearly bring forward retirement income, knocking down your tax profile after the year 2001 and reducing the double-tax bite. And the money from your plan can go into quality growth mutual funds, for example, which would yield you capital gains taxed at a far lower rate. Or you could invest to receive dividend income, further dropping your taxes.

This strategy can be used in combination with the other two after-RRSP options, which are annuities and RRIFs. With such a major tax change as the Seniors Benefit on the horizon, I can't stress enough the importance of anyone nearing age 60 getting financial advice now. The decisions you make will have a major impact on your future standard of living.

Or, go for cash for life

The second option is to use the money in your RRSP to buy an annuity from an insurance company, bank or trust. By giving over a lump sum of money, you get monthly cheques in return—for as long as you live (a life annuity), or for a defined period of time (fixed-term annuity).

The amount of money you receive will depend on your age, health, prevailing interest rates and life expectancy. The younger and healthier you are, the less you receive. With a life annuity, the payments continue until you die, unless you have a joint-and-last-survivor annuity, in which case payments continue until the last spouse expires. No payments are made into the estate or to beneficiaries.

With a fixed-term annuity, you usually get cheques until age 90, or you can base it on your spouse's age, if he or she is younger. Also

Source: *Today's Seniors*

available are "boutique" annuities, like ones indexed to inflation or a higher impaired annuity if you are in rough shape and likely to die sooner than the charts predict. And you can use non-RRSP money to purchase a prescribed annuity—which is a way of converting money in mutual funds or bonds, while leaving your RRSP assets to do what they really should, and that is . . .

Convert to a flexible RRIF

Consider a RRIF as a reverse RRSP; that is, you have to start taking money out. Contributions are no longer accepted. And after the first year, the amount you withdraw is determined by formula.

Of course, you pay tax on what's called the "minimum annual pay-out" (MAP). Taxes are not withheld by the bank or trust, as is the case for an RRSP, but the MAP is considered income, and your marginal rate applies. So, anyone with income of over $60,000 will lose half the amount withdrawn.

That's the bad news. The good news is a RRIF is as flexible and generous as an RRSP in its ability to allow the assets in there to grow and compound free of tax. So, you should have your RRIF set up as a self-directed fund and be following the same growth strategies as your RRSP did.

Since RRIFs were created in 1978, the rules have been changed several times to make them more effective:

- You can have as many RRIFs as you want, just like RRSPs. But— again like a retirement plan—one big self-directed one is best.

- The money no longer needs to be all taken out by age 90. Now a RRIF can be structured to give you income during your entire life.

- You can set up a RRIF at any age.

But the trade-off for this flexibility has been a higher required MAP in the early years of retirement. Here are the rules dictating how much money you have to withdraw.

Under the age of 69

Remember: You can set up a RRIF no matter what age you are, and the amount you must withdraw is less, the younger you are. You are also allowed to have the minimum payments based on your spouse's age— which is great if you married young. Just make sure you chose that option when the RRIF is first set up.

Here's the formula:

$$\frac{\text{Value of your RRIF}}{\text{90 minus your age (or your spouse's)}} = \text{Minimum payment}$$
$$\text{at beginning of year}$$

For example, if you are 65 and have $200,000 in your RRIF, then your minimum annual payment will be $200,000 divided by 90 minus 65 (which is 25), which equals $8,000. If your spouse is 55, then the MAP is equal to $200,000 divided by 90 minus 55 (35), which equals $5,714. Clearly, you are miles ahead in terms of deferring tax by having your spouse's age used instead of your own.

Over the age of 69

Although the 1996 budget dropped the age at which you have to convert your RRSP into a RRIF by two years, the formula for calculating minimum income (see above) stays the same until age 71.

After age 71, there is a specified percentage of your RRIF that must be taken as income each year. There is no getting around this, but by using the younger spouse's age, the MAP can be reduced, and more of your RRIF capital is preserved to keep on growing tax-free inside the fund.

Each year a new calculation is made by your bank, trust company or adviser to adjust the amount of income you must take in that year.

Here are the minimum payments, by age.

Age	Annual payment must be equal to this % of RRIF
71	7.38%
72	7.48
73	7.59
74	7.71
75	7.85
76	7.99
77	8.15
78	8.33
79	8.53
80	8.75
81	8.99
82	9.27
83	9.58
84	9.93
85	10.33
86	10.79
87	11.33
88	11.96
89	12.71
90	13.62
91	14.73
92	16.12
93	17.92
94 and over	20.00

You can see the tax bite grows steadily as you age, to the point when 20% of your assets have to be taken as income each year in your nineties. At that rate, the RRIF dwindles fast. But should you still be alive and kicking at that age, chances are your cash requirements will be very high—especially in the future, when more health care is privatized and the state can no longer afford subsidized institutional care.

That means a RRIF is important, but it should not be your only source of retirement income. So, past the age of 80 or so, it would make sense to take a chunk of RRIF money and convert it to a life annuity. That would bring down the minimum RRIF payments and give you an assured monthly cheque for life. But, there are other considerations if you are concerned about your estate.

When you die

If there's any good news about dying, this may be it: Money in a RRIF gives you better estate protection than an annuity, which usually ends when you do.

Always make it clear when you set up the RRIF who the beneficiary will be, and then back that up with a further declaration in your will. If you designate your spouse, then regular annual payouts can simply start flowing to him or her, or the spouse can collapse the plan, take all the money (and pay all the taxes) and go for a world cruise.

Alternatively, a younger spouse (under the age of 69) can roll the RRIF assets into his or her RRSP, or the RRIF can be collapsed and then restructured into a new RRIF, according to the spouse's wishes.

And if you do not name a beneficiary at all, the RRIF is cashed on your demise, with the money rolled into your estate and treated as income in that year. It's a good thing you won't be around to see that tax bill!

Chapter 4

What Happens if They Tax RRSPs?

This is a question I get asked a lot, especially at financial seminars after I present strategies for making the most of the RRSP rules as they currently stand. Many people are clearly worried about building up a highly visible nest egg that seems vulnerable to immediate attack by some future government.

The suspicion that there's a war on wealth in this country is shared by a lot of Canadians. And how can you blame them? Our top tax rate in this country is 15% higher than in the United States, and we start paying it around the $60,000 mark, while Americans don't get there until well over $200,000 is earned.

The reality is many people just don't trust Ottawa, which helps explain the recent fetish with offshore investment accounts (and Revenue Canada's vow to hunt them down).

Middle-aged, middle-class people probably have the most to lose over the next couple of decades. Today's retirees and the near-retired can count on government pension benefits. Younger generations are the most financially literate ever, and they have four decades to prepare. But poor Baby Boomers 15 or 20 years from retirement, with far too little saved and struggling within a restructuring economy, are sitting ducks for more government revenue grabs. And, yes, they will inevitably come.

But the threat of any future tax increases does not diminish the importance of RRSPs as they currently exist. Ottawa will continuously tinker with the rules, but I cannot foresee a major attack on personal retirement savings.

But there are clearly threats to the RRSP system. These, in my view are the Big Five.

THE ABILITY TO CARRY FORWARD UNUSED CONTRIBUTIONS COULD END

It's only a matter of time. It might take another budget, or maybe five, but it's clearly coming. There is over $130 billion in contributions Canadians have missed making, but could easily catch up on if they employed some of the strategies in this book.

If they did, the deficit would explode thanks to all those rebate cheques and lost government revenues. The hope of a balanced budget—which Ottawa clearly wants to showcase for the millennium—would be lost.

Besides, with the future of the Canada Pension Plan in doubt, political pressure is building in some social-activist circles to scale back on the breaks being given the "rich" people in the middle class who hide their wealth in RRSPs and thereby avoid paying their fair and moral share of taxes, or so the argument goes.

So, do not be surprised when the carry-forward provision is altered. It will either just be killed outright, with a return to pre-1991 rules that said make your annual contribution or lose it; or we'll go back to allowing a carry-forward for a defined number of years, as was the case before the 1996 federal budget.

In either case, if you have a carry-forward today, use it. If you lack the cash, borrow it. If you have other assets, make a contribution in kind, and get them into your self-directed plan. Any delay is a gamble you need not take.

Remember, your financial adviser can tell you how much you can put in, combining this year's contribution, the carry-forward and (if you haven't made it) your overcontribution.

RRSP CONTRIBUTIONS COULD GO FROM TAX DEDUCTIONS TO TAX CREDITS

This would be sneaky, and a heck of an effective way for the feds to reduce the revenue lost due to the current system. Today you are allowed to deduct the whole amount of your RRSP contribution from your taxable income. That directly reduces the amount of tax you pay and, in fact, the more money you make, the more tax you save.

Right now, people in the top tax bracket get back 53 cents on every dollar they contribute to their retirement plan, compared with 25 cents on the dollar for people earning less than $30,000.

Source: *The Financial Post*

If the contribution was treated as a credit, the refund for lower-income earners would remain about the same, but it would tumble for those making more. Those in the top tax bracket would see that 53-cent break fall to about 30 cents—and, yes, that would reduce the tax benefit by about half.

RRSP ASSETS COULD BE SUBJECT TO DIRECT TAXATION

This one has already been floated, in fact by Jim Peterson, current chairman of the House of Commons finance committee. He raised the trial balloon before the 1995 federal budget was brought down but, to his credit, Finance Minister Paul Martin didn't take the bait.

Not yet, anyway.

What Peterson mused on was a 1% annual tax on the assets of RRSPs with more than $500,000 in them. Politically, that has curb appeal, because half a million dollars sounds like a lot of money to most Canadians and 1% sounds like a very small tax.

But the implications are horrific. Such a tax would seriously compromise the whole intent of the system, erode investor confidence and rattle the financial markets. It would break faith with taxpayers and signal that the government simply cannot be trusted with long-term fiscal and social policy.

That, of course, is no reason it won't happen. But the bottom line is that even such a backward and myopic move would not overcome the advantages of contributing heavily to an RRSP.

CONTRIBUTION LEVELS COULD BE REDUCED

They already have been—several times, in fact. The old rules said we should have been at the annual $15,500 level by now, but here we are, frozen at a maximum of $13,500 well into the new century.

Today's rules still say the limit will be raised when the current freeze ends, and eventually indexed to inflation. But don't bet your spouse on it. The fact is only a tiny percentage of Canadians actually qualify to make the top contribution, so dropping it would not have major consequences while sending out the desired political signal that those rich layabouts who run companies and create jobs have to pay more.

If that's you, make sure you are maxing out every year you can.

THE SAVINGS PERIOD COULD BE CUT

It's already started, of course. The 1996 budget reduced the age at which you can no longer contribute to your RRSP by two years, from 71 to 69.

The implications of that are large, indeed. It removed from everyone the potential to shelter from tax tens of thousands of dollars. It shaved 24 months off the time you can save for retirement. And it accelerated by the same time the date at which you have to start collapsing your savings.

Now that the age has been changed once, it can be changed again. In fact, it's possible the RRSP contribution cut-off age and the official retirement age might soon be the same—say, 67.

Let me make it clear these are just possibilities. I have no hard evidence any of these threats will come to pass, but then, nobody expected the last budget to attack RRSPs as it did; gut future pension benefits for middle-class people; eviscerate labour-sponsored venture-capital funds; or wipe out existing tax breaks.

Ironically, one of the most foresightful things the national government can do is to encourage more private savings and future financial independence. Our troubling demographics are there for everyone to see. The best way of dealing with the coming retirement crisis is to allow Canadians to build their savings. And the best tool for that is—yes, the RRSP.

If you agree, don't be shy about saying so.

Chapter 5

Winning RRSP Strategies

It's inevitable. Baby Boomers are going to have to work longer.

—Demographer Robert Brown

Canada will have a crisis of poverty the likes of which it hasn't seen since the Depression. A lot of people are going to be hurting.

—Bea Lewis, Ontario Coalition of Senior Citizens' Organizations

It's time for government to set the stage for a coherent and strategic approach to the retirement of the baby boom. Review of all factors is likely to find there is a need to encourage and enable more private savings and rely less on government—a strategy opposite to the one that underpins these budget provisions.

—William Mercer Ltd. commentary on 1996 federal budget

There is no doubt in my mind that we are at a critical point for most Canadians. While the economy and financial markets are poised for stunning growth, most people don't see it and are not investing to take advantage of what will come. Media commentators ask how we can have record numbers of personal bankruptcies and record bank profits at the same time.

Seniors are worried about changes that will dramatically increase tax burdens within the next few years. Generation Xers are faced with the prospect of no pensions in their senior years and depression-like conditions in the middle of their working lives. And the Baby Boomers that most people think comprise one of the most-favoured generations ever are vastly unprepared for a retirement that's coming fast.

Record numbers of Canadians have been cashing in their RRSPs, and a staggering 52% of them are Boomers—under the age of 45.

What's wrong with this picture?

> *Simply put: There is nothing weak about the economy. In fact, the economic future is very bright. The problem is that Canadians are investing in the wrong ways, and in the wrong places. Too few are taking advantage of today's outstanding opportunities because they fear the future. Worse, they are not harnessing the power of the RRSP.*

Study the strategies I am presenting here and elsewhere in this book. Discuss them with your financial adviser, and if you don't have an adviser, then get one. Finally, do what most Canadians will not—take action, and implement these strategies, starting immediately. Never, never assume that in the years to come the government will be there to support you, or that future investments will make up for lost ground today. That's just not going to happen.

And the older you are, the more urgent it is. As I write this, most at risk are the Boomers, who must now be earning double-digit rates of return within their RRSPs for the next 15 years if they harbour a hope of maintaining a middle-class lifestyle. Most are not doing that right now, still wedded to the twin myths that: (a) retirement assets should be held in risk-free investments like GICs and (b) money ploughed into real estate is safe. Those who do not quickly shake those beliefs will end up both bitter and poorer.

Are you ready?

INVEST FOR GROWTH

RRSPs are not GICs. They are merely mechanisms for shielding your assets from tax. That means they are ideal for harbouring highly taxed assets like strip bonds. For example, a government bond paying 8% held for 30 years within an RRSP would give you double the return on the same bond held outside the plan—even assuming you paid the top marginal tax rate when you cashed out the RRSP.

In fact, an RRSP is so effective at maximizing the yield on such an investment that—according to the calculations of Bruce Cohen, of *The Financial Post*—future tax rates could soar as high as 82% and you'd still be better off having money in an RRSP that was cashed out at the tax level.

JUST ARRIVED FROM PLUTO

Source: Anthony Jenkins, *The Globe and Mail*

So, Rule One is that assets which are most susceptible to tax should go into your RRSP first. That includes strip bonds, savings bonds, mortgages and GICs. And remember, strips always beat GICs because you get a better rate with less risk, and the ability to cash out at any time.

But don't stop there.

Growth investments, even with a lower tax profile than bonds and investment certificates, also belong in your RRSP. In fact, if you are a Baby Boomer like me or younger, it is essential you have growth-oriented assets in your plan. Because, if you do not, the chances of accumulating enough by retirement age wither quickly.

The best growth assets to have are stocks and mutual funds. How could you go wrong, for example, buying the shares of major Canadian banks? These companies are wildly profitable, with a stranglehold on the financial-services sector, a virtual monopoly on the domestic market, and growing international operations. I wouldn't be surprised to see the share price of all the banks double over the next five or six years.

And, of course, quality, equity-based mutual funds have been giving investors double-digit returns for most of the 1990s.

> *There is little reason to believe this won't continue and much to suggest the golden age of equities is just nicely under way, swollen by a river of money flowing out of low-yielding fixed-income investments; real-estate equity, which is giving zero rates of return; and the savings of the Boomers, who are growing desperate for high numbers.*

Mutual-fund assets increased by 25% in Canada during 1995, and even more in 1996. In the U.S. mutual funds topped $3 trillion for the first time last year. Some people worry that so much money is on the move and that a stock-market correction could cause an avalanche in the other direction. But with an aging North American population, the need for high rates of return will likely keep the bulk of investors in the market, and maybe even see them increasing their holdings when prices take the inevitable tumble.

Make sure you grab some of this growth. I fail to see the risk in buying and holding quality funds like Templeton Growth, Fidelity Growth America, Trimark, Investors U.S. Growth, C.I. Canadian Growth, 20/20 International value or many other quality funds.

The key here is to make sure you are a long-term investor, buying these funds and holding them for a minimum of 5 years—15 would be even better.

> *I believe there is virtually no down-side in the stock market, so long as an investment is held long enough.*

Take a look at any chart of the market over 15, 40 or 100 years and you can clearly see the trend for prices is higher. The smart money buys on weakness and sells only on necessity.

Over the last three decades, the Toronto Stock Exchange TSE 300 Index has yielded an average of almost 10%—beating out every other asset class. And now that inflation has collapsed and interest rates are in a steady long-term decline, equities will attract more interest, and the pressure for higher prices will increase.

Can you afford not to invest?

CATCH UP ON MISSED CONTRIBUTIONS—NOW

Considering that an RRSP is the best tax shelter in North America, it is shocking how few Canadians actually use it. Fewer than a third of the people who file tax returns make an RRSP contribution. Only 11% make their maximum contributions.

Why is that?

First, many people file tax returns just to qualify for various government benefits. They don't have any income. Others have just started working and don't qualify yet to open a plan. And then there are all those Canadians who are just slaves to their mortgages and do not realize how dangerous their financial lives are.

Millions of people in this country have savings, but they are not tax-sheltered in an RRSP. They pay far more tax than they need to, and are not enjoying full compounding of their investments. Others do not realize that contributing just $100 a month can result in a quarter-million-dollar RRSP in twenty-five years.

In any case the reality is grim: We have missed about $150 billion in past contributions—a huge sum that could vastly improve the retirements of many people. Total unused-contribution room is growing by leaps and bounds—it increased 57% between 1993 and 1995, and could peak at $200 billion this year, 1997. That means we are getting to the point at which the buildup is so huge it may never be realized.

Statistics Canada figures show that almost 80% of taxpayers are eligible to make an RRSP contribution—half of them of more than $2,500; 25% more than $4,000; and 3% above $10,000. The average age is pure Baby Boomer, 39, and 46% are women.

And as I argue elsewhere in this book, there is every reason to believe the current ability to catch up on missed contributions will be ended at some point—maybe some point very soon.

Why?

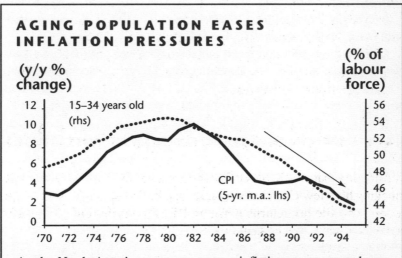

AGING POPULATION EASES INFLATION PRESSURES

As the North American economy ages, inflationary pressure drops. And when inflation falls, so do interest rates. The bad news for savers is rates are going to be low for a long, long time.

Source: Nesbitt Burns

Because if everyone were to do what I am suggesting, the federal deficit would blossom. Ottawa's secret goal of getting to a balanced budget—no operating deficit—by the year 2000 would be lost. And that is why one of these next few budgets will clearly signal that lost contributions will stay lost.

That means it is imperative to catch up now, while you still have the opportunity of retracing lost ground back to 1991. If you are reading this book during "RRSP season," 1997—those few weeks of the year prior to the beginning of March—then this is what I want you to do:

• make your full 1996 contribution; then

• make the allowable overcontribution of $2,000, if you have not already done so; then

• catch up on all your missed past contributions.

You can find out that amount in one of two ways. First, get your financial adviser to do it for you, because that's part of the normal job he or she should be doing. Or, you can call Revenue Canada and find out yourself. Here's how:

Look in the blue pages of your local phone directory under "Government of Canada." Find the "Revenue Canada" section, then "Tax Services" under that. Listed below will be the "TIPS Automated" number—"TIPS" stands for "Tax Information Phone Service."

Call and answer the computer-generated questions. You'll need to have your birth date, social insurance number and last year's income tax return. The TIPS machine will end up telling you what your current RRSP contribution limit is, along with the amount of missed contributions.

Now go to your bank, trust, broker or adviser's office. Open a self-directed RRSP and put all that money in, investing in a mix of government bonds, stocks and mutual funds that suits your goals, making sure that 20% of it is in foreign content—and I'd suggest international stock funds.

And what if you don't have that much extra money?

Then borrow it. As mentioned elsewhere, you can get an RRSP loan just about anywhere, and at prime. If you deal with a financial adviser, in many cases he or she has access to capital at even cheaper rates. Typically, you don't need to start repaying it until after you get your tax refund, and that refund should be used to pay down a good portion of the loan.

Borrowing for an RRSP contribution makes perfect sense, especially at a time like this, when interest rates are at generationally low levels

Canadians rush to plow cash into RRSPs

Banks extend hours to deal with last-minute flurry

BY SUSAN BOURETTE
The Globe and Mail

Canadians are rushing in at the 11th hour to plow funds into regis-

It is much the same story at Bank of Montreal's main Vancouver branch, which is keeping its doors open until 7 p.m. tonight.

Taxpayers can contribute up to 18 per cent of their previous year's income to a maximum of $14,500 for 1995 and $13,500 for 1996 — an

Will we never learn? Making an RRSP contribution the way most people do—in the first two months of the next calendar year—means a whole year of tax-free compounding is lost.

Source: *The Globe and Mail*

and the return on financial assets is so high. It is a rare opportunity for catching up. Do it now.

CONTRIBUTE EARLY

Every year people make the same mistake. They contribute to an RRSP exactly 12 months later than they should have. And, man, do they ever pay for it.

The rules say we all have until 60 days after the end of a taxation year to make a contribution that can be used to reduce taxes in that year. That's why every January and February have been turned into a RRSP orgy as the sellers of retirement funds remind us that this big deadline is looming. Sure, it is a good thing to put money into a plan at any time, but by always making that contribution at the very end of the allowable period, instead of at the beginning, you lose an entire year in which that money could have been growing tax-free.

Don't think that matters much?

Putting in $3,500 at the beginning of the year, instead of at the end of the year in a mutual fund earning 10% (and most are doing much better than that) will give you almost $60,000 more after 30 years.

That, of course, is money for nothing—no additional contribution. No borrowing. No pain. No risk. All you have done to earn it is change the day on which you made the contribution.

So why is it that so many people wait until the very last few weeks to contribute? Because they are victims of the media hype surrounding RRSPs during the winter months; because many worry about money, but do nothing until they're pushed; and because they don't know how easy it is to make an extra $60,000.

So, contribute to your RRSP early in the year, by all means, but do it a year early. And you can also get on a monthly plan to have RRSP money debited from your paycheque or chequing account on a regular basis. After a short while, it becomes like a car loan—something you don't even miss. But the benefits down the road can be stunning.

The good news is more and more investors are opting for this route. Thank goodness—an outbreak of sanity.

MAXIMIZE YOUR CASH FLOW

One chronic complaint I hear from people who miss making their RRSP contributions is that there's no money left at the end of the month to put towards retirement.

Well, we can fix that using this strategy.

Most middle-class people work for paycheques. Federal and provincial income taxes are deducted from those cheques by employers who, by law, have to remit the money on a regular basis.

Most people think there's just nothing they can do about this. But they're wrong. You can reduce the tax being withheld and maximize your cash flow. The key is making that RRSP contribution either at the beginning of the taxation year, or in monthly instalments.

This way you can increase your cash flow by reducing your paycheque taxes. Instead of waiting for a year for that RRSP tax refund cheque, you get it every pay period.

Here's what to do:

• Make your whole yearly contribution in January, borrowing the money if you have to, or

• Set up monthly contributions to your plan, using preauthorized withdrawals from your chequing account, just the way you would with car payments.

• Now call the local district taxation office of Revenue Canada (the number is in the blue pages of the phone book under "Government of Canada") and ask for the phone number for Source Deductions. These are the folks your employer sends the money to that is deducted from your pay.

- Call Source Deductions and tell them you want your withholding tax adjusted because you have made or are making RRSP-contribution payments. Tell them you want a Tax Deduction Waiver. They'll ask for your estimated income for this year, and your expected deductions, and you will need to provide proof of the RRSP contribution.

- Revenue Canada will consider this, then, when approved, send the waiver to your employer, who can reduce the amount of tax taken off your cheque. The whole process takes about a month, and you have to do this every year in order to get the tax break.

- Now, your paycheque is going to be fatter. So don't squander it on incidentals. You could take that money and simply increase your mortgage payments, shortening the time before it's completely paid off (so you can replace it with a tax-deductible investment mortgage).

Or, that extra money would be ideal to purchase mutual-fund units on a monthly basis, again through preauthorized debits you will never miss. A few years of doing that, and you'll be astonished at how much farther ahead you are.

The bottom line here is pretty simple: Either you are a serious, long-term, dedicated RRSP contributor, or you are gambling with the future. Amateur investors line up in the snow on the last day of February to put money into an RRSP investment they barely understand.

Pros like you set up a yearly program with a financial adviser, and then reap the benefits: more compound income from contributing early; more after-tax income to invest; a much larger portfolio thanks to a disciplined approach.

It's not as sexy as winning the lottery or being the first to invest in Bre-X, but it's a heck of a lot more certain. Sure money can be pretty sexy, too.

LOAD UP THE LESS-TAXED SPOUSE

Use RRSPs to get as many assets as possible into the hands of the least-taxed spouse before retirement. Recent budget changes have made income-splitting more important than ever because pension-benefit clawbacks are about to be based on family, not individual, income.

The impact is stunning. Today a couple can have income of $167,000 before all their GIS and Old Age payments are taxed back. Under the Seniors Benefit, which will replace GIS and OAS, total clawback is based on joint income—of just $78,000, which is less than half that allowed under the current system.

And when the Seniors Benefit takes effect in 2001, retirees will face double taxation on their income—of between 42 and 78 cents of every dollar. That means it will be critical for couples to have their incomes as levelled out as possible, so both are taxed at the lowest applicable rate.

Is this a pain and unfair to folks who have been diligent in saving money for their old age? Of course it is, but always remember this:

> *Seniors are sitting ducks for increased government taxation—especially well-off seniors who, ironically, were the ones who prepared for retirement. Clawbacks of pension benefits will only increase. The best defence is to even out income flow between you and your spouse. Start doing that now, no matter how far off retirement is.*

The best and easiest way is with spousal RRSPs. As outlined in Chapter 3, in the section on spousal plans, you can contribute as much as you want, up to your limit (this year's contribution plus past unused ones plus the overcontribution), to your spouse's RRSP. This money becomes your spouse's property, so long as it's left in the plan for three years. And your contributing money to the spousal plan doesn't prevent your spouse from also contributing to a separate personal plan. You don't even need to be married—common-law is okay, but (so far) you do have to be of the opposite sex.

The tax savings in retirement can be significant. Remember how income is taxed, for example in B.C. and Ontario:

• Up to $28,000 income, pay tax at 27%;

• Every dollar above that is taxed at 41%; and

• Above $63,000, kiss away $51 of every $100 in income.

So, let's say through spousal RRSPs you were able to each take an income of $28,000 from retirement plans, instead of one spouse making $56,000. You'd pay 10% less income tax and give up far fewer pension benefits.

Unfortunately many of today's retired Canadians are in a very unhappy position of having virtually all family income flow through the hands of just one spouse. This is the legacy of the way families used to operate—Dad went to work for years and ended up with a company pension and investment assets while Mom raised kids, worked in the community and ended up with no income stream.

Today they pay vastly more than another couple with equal income but split between them. Fair? No, it's not fair. And it won't be getting fairer any time soon. But you can avoid the situation.

Spousal RRSPs are one way. Paying your less-taxed spouse's taxes is another. Paying your spouse or children a salary is also permitted, along with bankrolling a spouse's business so that all profits are attributed to him or her, not to you.

For more income-splitting techniques, consult your financial adviser. You'll also find some strategies in the current edition of my book *2015: After the Boom*.

MAKE THE OVERCONTRIBUTION

You are allowed to contribute up to $2,000 more into your plan than the rules normally allow. Do it now before this provision becomes history in some budget.

There are several reasons why:

- First, it's hard enough getting enough money into your RRSP where it grows tax-free, so even though you don't get a tax break for the overcontribution, it's still worth sheltering the money.

- This is the Nineties, which means your job could evaporate tomorrow. So carrying around an extra $2,000 in your RRSP is a good idea because, should you get laid off and not have enough earned income to make an RRSP contribution next year, you can use the two grand instead.

- If you have a dependant aged 19 or older, make the overcontribution in his or her name if the child does not have earned income and can't contribute to his or her own plan.

    You don't get a tax deduction, but when your son or daughter reaches age 59, the $2,000 could have turned into $90,000. Demand that the kid buy you a Porsche.

- Or, if you are retired but still have earned income (like from a rental house), make the overcontribution. So long as you continue to have earned income, you can claim the deduction yearly at the rate of 18% of income, until the $2,000 is exhausted. Ditto for a spousal plan.

GET AN INTEREST-FREE LOAN

This is a strategy only for first-time home buyers who can withdraw up to $20,000 each ($40,000 for a couple) to use as a down-payment on a home—new or resale.

It is, in effect, an interest-free and tax-free loan from your RRSP, which has to be paid back in equal instalments over 15 years. Miss a payment and it becomes taxable as part of your income in that year. You have at least two years before the repayments have to start.

But be wary.

Given the long-term decline in residential real-estate values, it probably does not make any sense to take money out of your RRSP to buy a home—certainly not while financial markets are showering double-digit rates of return on mutual-fund investors.

Critics have always said the Home Buyers' Plan corrupted the spirit of the RRSP program, and I now agree. But in the true spirit of that corruption, first-time home buyers might as well take advantage of loopholes that were never intended.

Here goes:

- If you are a couple in the 40% tax bracket with $20,000 saved for a down-payment, along with built-up, missed RRSP contributions, then make those contributions now.

- Then go house-hunting, making sure you do not close a deal prior to 90 days after you made the RRSP contribution.

- Cash in the RRSPs, tax-free, under the Home Buyers' Plan.

- And add to that the $8,000 Ottawa sent you in tax refunds because you contributed to your retirement (which you actually spent on a house). Now you have $28,000 to put down, and a smaller mortgage.

- The $20,000 will have to be paid back into your RRSP, starting in the year 2000 at the rate of $1,300 a year.

SELL YOURSELF YOUR OWN ASSETS

So many people miss making an RRSP contribution because they don't have enough cash saved up by the time the annual deadline passes.

Silly them!

> *You don't need money to make an RRSP contribution.*
> *All you need are some assets. The government will*
> *pay you for selling yourself what you already own.*

The rules are crystal clear. You are allowed to move assets that are currently subject to tax into your tax-free RRSP, to the limit of your annual contribution, and then claim this as a tax deduction just as if you'd contributed saved-up cash.

It's called "contributions in kind," and it's a terrific way for people to catch up on their tax-sheltered retirement savings. And it's also a strategy that every investor should employ to reduce the tax load. Every year Dorothy and I move as many of our investments as possible into RRSPs, getting those government bonds and mutual funds under the protective, tax-free bubble.

Remember the example I used earlier of a person with savings bonds but no RRSP—we used this strategy to turn $7,000 into $39,000:

- We opened a self-directed RRSP.

- Then we transferred the bonds into the plan, and cashed them.

- Next, we borrowed $2,800 from the bank, which was paid off in full two months later with the tax-refund cheque we got for transferring the CBSs into the RRSP.

- Now we had enough in the RRSP to purchase a Government of Ontario strip bond maturing in 2010, with a maturity value of $39,000. It can be held to maturity or sold off earlier for a capital gain if interest rates drop.

> *This would be outrageous if it were not perfectly*
> *legal. And the shame of it is that most Canadians*
> *are completely unaware this kind of thing can be*
> *done with a phone call.*

How many people are out there with no sheltered retirement savings plans, and at the same time have money in GICs, savings bonds, term deposits, savings accounts and other brain-dead investments that they could be leveraging higher, tax-free?

Do you? And are you going to do something about it? Today?

Some of the assets that qualify to put into your self-directed RRSP

Canada Savings Bonds	GICs
Provincial Savings Bonds	Mutual-fund units
Cash	Labour-fund units
Corporate bonds	Limited partnership units
Government of Canada bonds	Stocks
Provincial government bonds	Mortgages
Term deposits	Small-business shares

Some assets that don't qualify

Foreign currency	Gold, silver
Real estate	Commodities

HOLD YOUR OWN MORTGAGE

As outlined in the section "Your RRSP and your real estate," in Chapter 3, it is possible to put your own residential mortgage inside your RRSP and make mortgage payments to yourself.

Let's review why this is a cool idea: It amounts to a regular, forced transfer of wealth from your income stream into your RRSP. By setting it up properly, you can exceed your annual allowed-contribution limits. And you don't end up making the bank richer.

The process is a bit complicated. You will need to work it out with a competent financial adviser, and it does cost money—about a thousand bucks—to set it up, and then several hundred dollars a year to administer.

You also need a lot of cash, or cashable investments, in your RRSP— enough to write a new mortgage that will replace the one you already have in place. (And don't forget that wriggling out of a bank mortgage before its term expires can be difficult and costly. Early payoff will cost you three months' interest, or the difference between your existing mortgage rates and current ones over the term remaining—whichever is more.)

Of course, you also need a self-directed RRSP. It will lend enough money to discharge the existing mortgage, replace it with a new one, and take title to the property (that means you need a lawyer, too).

Once that is in place, you make regular mortgage payments every week or month into your RRSP. As I mentioned, Revenue Canada dictates that the mortgage rate must be comparable with existing current rates. That means you can't issue yourself a 2% home loan. But then, you don't want to do that. In fact, you want to give yourself the highest possible mortgage rate—because the idea is to use this device to squeeze as much of your income as possible into the RRSP. This is not a device for making real estate more affordable. Instead, it's a strategy to bloat your retirement savings.

You also have to insure the mortgage, and you must qualify for it financially, just as if you were going to the bank. Finally, the whole thing has to be administered by an unrelated lender (typically a trust company). And if you don't carefully follow all the rules, Revenue Canada will simply disqualify the deal and your taxes will throb.

The bottom line, however, is that this is very much worth doing as an aggressive RRSP strategy. And it makes even more sense when your RRSP lends out money to finance an income-generating property, like a rental house. Then the interest payments you are making into your own RRSP are deductible from your taxable income. Have you heard of double taxation? This is the opposite.

LIBERATE YOUR REAL ESTATE

In the first half of your life, it makes a lot of sense to acquire and pay off real estate. In the second half, use real estate as a tool to gain more financial assets (as in the example above), or as a source of equity to invest in financial assets. (Never forget that the long-term investment trend with an aging population and lots of house-rich and cash-poor Boomers is from real assets to financial ones. That's why real estate has tanked in the Nineties, and mutual-fund assets hit a new record high every month.)

Your RRSP can certainly help.

If you have a paid-up, mortgage-free home, then it represents a lot of money—often hundreds of thousands of dollars—typically earning peanuts (if anything) in capital appreciation. At least a portion of this money could, and should, be out working in the global economy, where it can easily be making double-digit returns.

That's why it pays to remortgage a home, invest the money in mutual funds and create a tax-deductible mortgage. Because the proceeds of the mortgage are used to buy financial assets yielding a greater return than the cost of the mortgage, you get to write off the interest payments from your taxable income. In tax terms, it's considered not a mortgage, but an investment loan.

But it sure looks and smells like a mortgage to your RRSP.

So, if you have enough cash in your retirement plan (or cashable assets), you can take over that mortgage (subject to the conditions mentioned above) and start enjoying several benefits, namely:

- Liberating your previously locked-in and underperforming equity so it can go out into the world and multiply, while

- Creating a sizeable tax deduction and increasing your after-tax income, while

- Giving you a greater ability to shovel money into your RRSP through the vehicle of an RRSP mortgage.

BOUCHARD-PROOF YOUR WEALTH

> *Canada, for a long time, would be weaker than it would be as a united country.*
> —*John McCallum, Chief Economist, Royal Bank*

As I write this, the tug-of-war goes on between Ottawa and Quebec City as the feds and the separatists play their elaborate public-relations game for the support of a confused electorate. It's impossible to know what the ultimate outcome will be—a stronger Canada, a fractured one or another 20 years of uncertainty that will keep investors away, the dollar down and interest rates higher than they'd otherwise need be.

Above all, financial markets hate uncertainty and, for the last 17 years, that's what they've got from Canada. Some analysts believe any kind of a resolution to this—even outright Quebec separation—would be better than the current situation. In fact, a 1996 report by CIBC Wood Gundy economists Jeff Rubin and Peter Buchanan argued a Canada without Quebec would be better off financially. But others, like Bank of Montreal economist Tim O'Neill, say a split would result in sharply higher rates, a slide in the dollar's value, lower business and consumer confidence, and probably a recession.

In any case, let's face the facts: The bad guys almost won the October 30, 1995, referendum. The next time we might not be as lucky. And even the mere announcement of the next referendum date will be enough to spook financial markets, torpedo the loonie and drive a lot of naive investors for the exits as the value of stocks and mutual funds temporarily dips.

We already have experienced this.

Terrified investors dumped millions of dollars in stock and bond funds in the weeks and days running up to the October referendum, even when many of them were selling at a loss. Hardest hit were the no-load funds, of course, because investors don't face redemption charges or have to forgo commissions paid on purchasing the fund (and this is why no-load-fund investors usually have far poorer returns than the buy-and-hold load-fund crowd).

Hardest hit was the Bank of Montreal's family of First Canadian Funds, followed by Altamira, while many load funds increased their total assets in October 1995.

NO-LOAD FUNDS LOSE OUT

	Assets $ millions	Oct. Sales $ millions (redemptions)
As of Oct. 31, 1995		
Investors Group	18,805	26,491
Trimark	12,453	224,997
Royal Funds	11,779	(48,810)
Mackenzie	10,815	150,568
CIBC	6,291	(63,092)
Fidelity	5,914	(12,684)
T-D	5,858	46,569
Templeton	5,770	117,725
Altamira	4,923	(101,262)
MD Management	4,490	19,165
C.I. Funds	4,487	18,263
Bank of Montreal	4,472	(118,227)
AGF	4,377	30,609
CT Funds	4,112	(19,691)

And the day after the referendum, when financial markets rallied dramatically, all those people who sold decided to buy back again—in keeping with the typical Canadian investment strategy of waiting for a crisis so we can sell low and then buy high! The day after the referendum each major bank no-load firm saw about $50 million flow back. Investors Group witnessed more than $20 million go from cash into equity and bond funds. At the Bank of Commerce, $47 million coursed into equities and bonds, while at Altamira, president Philip Armstrong told *The Financial Post* it was "wall-to-wall buying" as the company received more than 2,000 phone calls.

This, of course, is panic, knee-jerk investing. And it just about guarantees you will lose money.

There is a way to partially protect yourself from the fray, and that is to make sure you are completely topped up on foreign content in your RRSP.

Rich people know this. A study done last year by Environics for the Royal Bank showed foreign investment and wealth go hand in hand. Among the country's top 10% by income, 68% own some form of global investments, including mutual funds, real estate, stocks and bonds.

As the Royal's Michael Lagopoulos summarized, "The wealthier the individual, the more likely they are to have international assets."

In sharp contrast, although almost 70% of wealthy people have international investments, just 28% of all Canadians surveyed by Royal Trust intended to put RRSP money into foreign holdings. This could be due to the perception that foreign investments are riskier than Canadian ones, when, in fact, it's a lot safer to be diversified among several countries than entirely invested in any one.

As the Environics survey showed, the more money people have, the more they go global:

NET WORTH

	Under $250K	$250K–$500K	Over $500K
Global Investments	57%	74%	78%
International Mutual Funds	31%	46%	55%
International Stocks	22%	27%	37%
Foreign Real Estate	13%	24%	24%

Market carnage over Quebec

C$ loses nearly a cent, TSE suffers biggest one-day loss in six years

Lest we forget. It will happen again, just like this, as the next referendum approaches. But there are ways to Bouchard-proof your investments without converting your money.

Source: *The Financial Post*

As we've discussed, the rules allow you to have 20% of your total RRSP book value in foreign content. That could be yen-denominated bonds, international mutual funds or foreign stocks.

Until recently, investors could include shares only of companies listed on stock exchanges in the United States, Britain or France. Now the list has been expanded to include 12 other exchanges, including hot ones like Hong Kong, Tokyo and Mexico City. Of course, these foreign investments also grow free from tax within your RRSP, and earn you a rebate cheque from the government for buying them.

The Canadian dollar has eroded steadily over the last few years, against both the American dollar and other major currencies, like the yen. With the Quebec situation unresolved, with the spectre of another referendum, and with the country still adding tens of billions to its debt each year, the loonie is at risk.

More national-unity problems and the currency could easily test its all-time low of just over 69 cents U.S. If, in your mind, that is even a remote possibility, why not take action today to ensure a good chunk of your retirement assets goes up, not down, on the dollar's decline?

Every Canadian with assets should be doing the prudent thing: Reviewing your portfolio—now—with a financial adviser in order to Bouchard-proof what you own. If you like investing in fixed-income, then why not buy a Government of British Columbia or Ontario bond that pays you in yen? If you want to buy shares in the Royal Bank, why not go for preferreds that give you dividends in U.S. dollars? Why not seek out and invest in Canadian companies that earn most of their income offshore? Actions like these will help preserve your wealth when the separatists strike again.

CONTRIBUTE NOW, CLAIM IT LATER

This strategy allows people who know they will be making more money later to maximize their tax savings. Remember: The higher your earnings and your tax bracket, the more valuable an RRSP contribution is to you, because it is a tax deduction rather than tax credit. So, a $10,000 contribution in the highest tax bracket nets you a refund of $5,400, compared with $4,000 back if your income slipped by a few thousand dollars.

So, if you know your earnings will rise, then make the RRSP contribution today (so the money can compound free of tax), but just save the official tax receipt for later. There is nothing in the rules that says that receipt has to be attached to the annual tax return for the year in which the contribution was made.

This strategy will work for a salesperson in a cyclical industry (like real estate, for example) who wants to keep making RRSP contributions, but saves up the receipts to offset income earned in a good year. It will work for a graduating dentist or lawyer just starting to build a practice. Or a high-salaried woman on maternity leave.

In these instances the tax receipt will actually be worth more in tax savings later—so why not hang on? Just make sure you keep good records and, of course, don't lose the receipts. Getting a financial institution to reissue lost receipts is possible, but growing an oak tree is usually faster.

DIVERSIFY, DIVERSIFY, DIVERSIFY

The single greatest mistake Canadian investors make is trying to do their own financial planning. The second mistake flows out of the first, because most of us are wimps—and we attempt to avoid all risk. That's why most RRSPs end up in the bank and invested in GICs.

Big mistake. The worst investment you can make is a GIC. Interest rates are low, and going lower, while inflation, although moderate, is debilitating. The combination is deadly, especially for anyone like me—a Baby Boomer who needs to earn double-digit returns for the next 15 years.

GIC investors usually have no idea they can earn a much higher rate of return, while taking less risk, with a government strip bond. Even more important, most Canadians have no idea that few investments are safer over the long haul than the stock market. So, do not avoid stocks

THE MARCH PAST 5,000

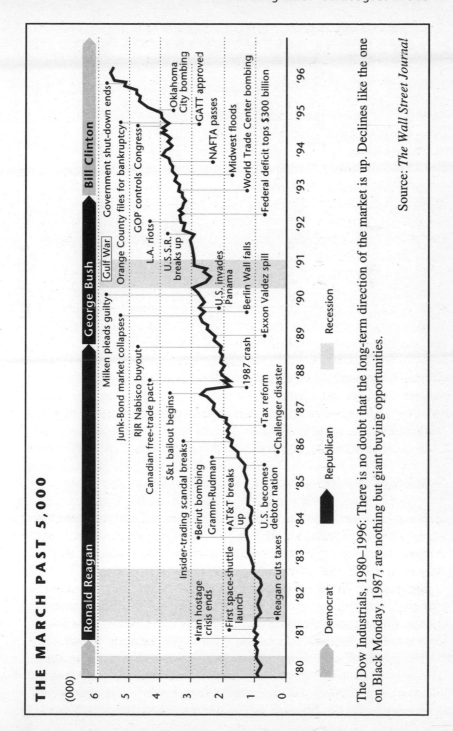

The Dow Industrials, 1980–1996: There is no doubt that the long-term direction of the market is up. Declines like the one on Black Monday, 1987, are nothing but giant buying opportunities.

Source: *The Wall Street Journal*

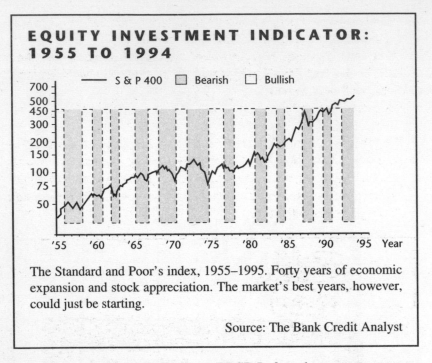

EQUITY INVESTMENT INDICATOR: 1955 TO 1994

The Standard and Poor's index, 1955–1995. Forty years of economic expansion and stock appreciation. The market's best years, however, could just be starting.

Source: The Bank Credit Analyst

or equity mutual funds inside your RRSP. In fact, the younger you are, the more you should have.

Take a look at the accompanying charts showing stock-market performance over the last 15 and the last 40 years. They show clearly that the long-term direction of stocks is up. Yes, there are periods of volatility after stock values rise too quickly, but those should just be viewed as buying opportunities.

Most Canadians have no idea the market is so safe. They do not realize stock values reflect technological advance, medical breakthroughs and economic expansion. If you have any faith in the future—and I have all kinds—then equities are the place to be. Just remember to buy quality stocks and mutual funds, and then forget about them. Go back and have a peak every five years or so.

And beware of "hot" stocks—the ones that get headline attention because they soar in value, making early investors rich. About the worst thing that has happened lately was the meteoric rise of Bre-X Minerals Ltd., which jumped from $2 a share to about $200 after the company made a huge gold discovery in Indonesia. That success had countless investors running around looking for the next junior-mining-stock miracle. But the odds were against them, as Bre-X was one in a million. So, a lot of people lost a lot of money on stocks like Cartaway Resources, which also soared, and then crumbled.

This is not investing. It's a crapshoot. Serious RRSP-equity investors should be buying high-quality growth stocks, especially when the market dips and they go on sale.

Remember the rules:

• Hot stocks get cold real fast. Usually by the time the newspapers notice a flaming stock, it has already peaked. If you insist on playing the game, though, make sure you keep an eye on what the stock promoters and insiders are doing with their holdings. When they start bailing out, go with them.

"This is Gerald Stump reporting live from Bay Street. Today, the stock market was hit very hard . . ."

Source: *The Toronto Star*

- You are always better to diversify. Don't invest in one stock, invest in ten. Don't invest in just one sector of the economy, buy several. The more you diversify, the less the risk.

- The best, easiest diversification comes through using mutual funds. You buy less risk along with superior management.

- Buy companies with proven track records. Your financial adviser can get you reams of information on a stock's history. The Internet is also an excellence source of performance data (see the "Internet Resources" section).

- Increase your holdings when stock values fall. Corrections are inevitable, and as I write this—with North American stock values at near-record levels—the mother of all corrections could well be around the corner. A dip of 15% would bring the TSE 300 down by the better part of 1,000 points—terrifying many novice market players but posing a huge buying opportunity for long-term investors.

Don't forget what history proves to us: There is no risk in the market for long-term investors. The market will continue to rise so long as mankind continues to advance. So far, I can't find any evidence a decline has begun.

Conventional investment logic is that the first things to go in your RRSP are the ones that are most heavily taxed when not tax-sheltered. That includes interest-bearing investments like bonds. Other investments, like stocks that pay you dividends or capital gains, should be held outside your RRSP. That way you don't lose the benefit of the dividend tax credit or more favourable treatment of capital gains.

If you have substantial assets, that rule holds. But most people don't have the wealth to justify two separate investment portfolios, so they should concentrate on building the RRSP and making sure its holdings are diversified. That will give you better returns with less risk.

> *Always be aware the greatest risk you face is not losing your money, but rather outliving it. Being content with a low-yielding GIC is false security. It's dangerous.*

Even beyond the age of 65, investors need to have a strong growth component to their retirement savings because the odds of living another 25 years are getting better every day. Over that period of time, nothing will perform better than equity-based mutual funds.

DON'T LABOUR OVER THE LABOUR FUNDS

A year ago it looked like it was impossible to lose making an RRSP investment in a labour-sponsored venture-capital fund. After all, the tax incentives were almost unbelievable: For investors in the top tax bracket, they got their 50% tax rebate, plus another 40% in federal and provincial tax credits.

The result was, for an investment of about $500, you could salt away a $5,000 asset in your retirement plan.

The labour funds were given this amazingly favourable treatment in order to encourage the growth of pools of capital that would flow out into the economy, into small and medium-sized enterprises, creating jobs. Nice theory, that was. And as a result of the tax break, during the 1996 RRSP season, investors gorged on these things, pumping millions in until the total pot stood at about $2 billion.

But all is not as it should be. Many funds have not been able to find companies to invest in, while others have non-existent or poor track records. Too many investors asked too few questions, caring only about the tax savings. As a result, they have ended up with bad investments.

Meanwhile a lot of critics sniped at the federal and provincial governments for using the tax system to distort people's investment decisions. In hindsight, the critics may have been right.

Consider the biggest labour fund, Working Ventures. It had expected to raise $150 million during the last RRSP season. Instead, it got $350 million. And four months later President Ron Begg had to tell a busy roomful of reporters that because the fund had swollen to more than $850 million—while only $170 million had actually been invested in businesses—new unit sales were being cut off for a year. Meanwhile the fund will probably pay out tens of millions of dollars in penalties because it did not do what it was supposed to—invest more in the economy.

Are labour funds a good investment?

Not any more. At least not most of them. The main reason is that shortly after last RRSP season, all the rules changed in subsequent federal and provincial budgets. The main changes came on March 6, when Finance Minister Paul Martin announced that:

- The federal tax credit was being reduced from 20% to 15%;

- The maximum share purchase eligible for the tax credit was being reduced from $5,000 to $3,500;

- The minimum holding period for labour fund shares was being increased from five to eight years, including for seniors and retirees.

- The ability to double-dip was being ended. Investors would no longer be able to redeem shares at the end of the holding period, and then immediately reinvest the money to get a new set of tax credits. Under the new rule, an investor has to wait two years past the year of redemption before being able to invest again and get a tax break. That effectively quashed what had looked like a promising strategy for seniors: Recycling their labour-fund shares every two years to keep loading up on those delicious tax credits.

Other jurisdictions, like Ontario, have followed suit with budget measures stripping away the funds' tax incentives. So now investors who bought units have to decide what course of action to take when they are eligible to sell.

In most cases, I'd recommend selling, because most of the funds are losers. But with Working Ventures, I am still hopeful it will prove to be a worthwhile investment—but long-long-term. The other winner is the Canadian Medical Discoveries Fund, run by Dr. Calvin Stiller and administered by Talvest Fund Management. It has invested in high-growth companies in the biotechnology sector, and so far has returned a decent yield to its shareholders.

With an aging population and an overwhelmed health-care system, the Medical Discoveries Fund has an excellent future and wise investors will want to have a piece of it.

As for the rest of them, bail out when you can.

PROTECT YOURSELF FROM CREDITORS

You may be shocked to learn that your RRSP assets are not protected by federal law from creditors. In fact, your investment can be at risk in several ways;

- If your marriage breaks up, provincial law will allow your ex-spouse to make a claim against your RRSP assets. In general, you will lose half.

- If the financial institution holding your RRSP goes belly-up, like Confederation Life did, you lose your assets beyond the insured limit of $60,000 for cash, GIC, term deposits and so on.

- If you die owing Revenue Canada money for unpaid taxes, your RRSP can be opened under the Income Tax Act, allowing the feds to get their money.

- If you go bankrupt, creditors could get a court order against your RRSP if the money you put in there over the last few years could have been used to pay off bills.

These are some of the threats you face, and there are always new attempts going on to crack into the pool of RRSP capital. It is a sorry reality that no federal law gives a consistent level of protection from creditors to RRSP investors across the country. Various provincial governments have tried—for example, in British Columbia, provincial law excludes RRSPs from an estate if the planholder had designated a beneficiary.

And this is exactly what you should do, wherever you live. Name your spouse as the beneficiary on your retirement plan for several reasons—to increase protection from creditors, to allow transfer of the RRSP assets upon death to the spouse and to avoid probate fees.

Finally, if you think you'll have problems with creditors in the future—or you just want to be as safe as possible—use a spousal RRSP to harbour your assets (as long as your spouse isn't on the run from the law). Assets put into a spousal plan become the possession of your spouse. RRSPs with life insurance companies are also protected from creditors.

TRACKING THE COMMON WISDOM

The most important thing you can do when investing your RRSP money is to make sure you maintain a long-term view. Most people don't. They assume today's reality will dictate future situations. But history tells us otherwise. For example, at the very height of the last real-estate boom, many people thought it would last forever. Today, equities and mutual funds are all the rage.

Consider the results of two *Business Week* polls done seven years apart:

If you had to choose the one investment that you think would be the best right now, which would it be?

	1989	1996
Real Estate	40%	25%
Mutual Funds	8%	24%
Common Stock	5%	10%

The shift away from real assets, including real estate, will only continue as the North American population ages. Billions of dollars will flow into equities and funds for more than a decade, pushing their valuations higher. More and more people will wake up to the fact the single best strategy is for them to drain out the equity in their homes while financial institutions are still making home-equity loans.

In the future, selling a suburban house could be simply impossible. The trend is already taking hold in the United States, where home-ownership levels for young people—under 34—are plunging.

As American University professor Peter Chinloy has said, "My guess is that younger people have seen the relatively low appreciation levels for real estate, and are holding more of their assets in stocks and bonds."

U.S. National Association of Realtors chief economist John Tucillo says that when the big price drop comes, there's little doubt what kind of housing will be hardest hit: "Undistinguished, middle-class suburban properties."

So this is a time for middle-aged investors to cash out real estate, or at least to use the equity they have built up to acquire financial assets.

But will those financial assets—stocks, bonds, mutual funds—tank in the future the way real estate is now? Anything is possible, but it's unlikely unless there's a bout of hyperinflation in the decades to come. That could be triggered by a debt crisis or a major international armed conflict or a civil war in Russia. In circumstances like those, people with their wealth in oil and gold would win, while the stock market collapsed.

In any case, unwavering demographics would still dictate tough times for real estate, which dances only to one beat: Supply and demand.

> *Right now the superior investment strategy is a*
> *dramatic move into financial assets; with a 10%*
> *inflation hedge against calamity through vehicles*
> *like an oil and gas fund, and a steady reduction in*
> *real-estate equity.*

WEALTH WITHOUT RISK: STRIP BONDS

> *Any Canadian with any of his or her RRSP assets in*
> *a guaranteed investment certificate (GIC) is making*
> *a big mistake. Interest rates are low, and going*
> *lower. Your investment is locked up for years.*
> *There's no potential of a capital gain.*

Why would people put their money in a GIC? There's only one possible answer: They think it's safe.

Well, there is an even safer place for retirement money that offers huge advantages over a GIC: strip bonds.

- Strips pay more interest.

- They are cashable anytime.

- They are free of risk. There is no limit similar to the $60,000 insurance threshold for GICs.

- They go up in value when interest rates go down, giving a capital gain.

- They sell at a deep discount to face value.

- And when safely tucked into your self-directed RRSP, they are virtual money machines—doubling or tripling your investment in a defined period of time.

Why doesn't everyone have strips? Because they don't sell them at most banks, so all those people trading growth for risk-free GICs are simply not being made aware of the strip-bond alternative.

You ought to be buying strips at regular times, and stagger their maturities. That way, in retirement, you'll have bonds maturing every year. Your income needs will be met, and you'll get the satisfaction of knowing that for every dollar you plopped down years earlier, you'll be getting three or four back—thanks to our indebted federal and provincial governments and their agencies and Crown corporations.

I think every RRSP ought to contain some government bonds. And let's not confuse these with Canada Savings Bonds or provincial copycats, like Ontario Savings Bonds. Those are tepid little investments, scarcely better than GICs, bought by people who actually think they are investing. Poor souls.

No, real government bonds are different, but as accessible as one phone call to your independent financial adviser. And, like GICs and CSBs, bonds are categorized as being "fixed-income," because they pay a predetermined amount of interest when held to maturity. But unlike GICs and CSBs, strip bonds fluctuate in value daily, rising or falling in reverse to interest rates, and they can be bought or sold at any time, no matter what maturity date they carry.

So, what is a government strip bond?

It starts life as a regular government bond issued by Ontario or Alberta or B.C. (or other bodies like Ontario Hydro or the Export Development Corporation) as part of the ongoing process of financing government spending.

Regular bonds pay investors interest, usually twice a year (although some pay monthly), so they are good for people looking for a steady, guaranteed income.

But brokers can take the bonds and separate them into two bits—the interest coupons and the principal of the bonds. As an investor, you can buy either the coupons, which will then also give you income on a regular basis (but no payout at the end), or you can buy the bond itself (which is stripped of interest—giving rise to the term, "strip" bond), which will pay you this way:

- face value on the day of maturity, or

- whatever the market value is on whatever day prior to maturity that you decide to sell.

Strip bonds are also issued by corporations, but they are not as secure as government strips because they're backed by corporate assets, not the power of taxation.

And that power to tax is exactly what gives strip bonds their security. It's as close to a complete guarantee as you are ever going to get with an investment. Often during my financial seminars someone will ask, "But what if the government is broke and defaults on its bonds in future years?"

Sure, that could happen. And in that case, the strip-bond investor would lose. But if a Canadian government ever defaulted on a bond issue, that would pretty well be the end of the Canadian dollar—including the ones in your GIC. In such a circumstance you could forget about the Canada Deposit Insurance Corporation refunding your money. It would be swept away in an instant.

So, because the bond is stripped of its interest coupons, it does not pay you interest. It's a residual bond, also called a "zero coupon" bond in the United States. And because it pays no interest, you buy it at a big discount to its face value. That means you can leverage a big payout years later with a much smaller amount of money now. The longer the period until the bond matures, the bigger the discount. And the higher the yield on the bond, the cheaper it is to buy.

Here's an example: In May 1994 I bought a Government of Ontario strip bond that matures on February 18, 2002. The annual yield was good at the time—8.86%, and on maturity day that bond will be worth $194,000 inside my RRSP. But the actual cost to buy it was $100,412, which worked out to be $51.75 for every $100 worth of bond. In effect, I was arranging to double my money in less than eight years—without risk.

By investing $100,412 I will receive $93,588 more than I paid in 7.7 years. Where else can you get a yield like that, guaranteed by the government?

Now some people will tell you these strip bonds are volatile and risky because the market price fluctuates as interest rates rise and fall. It certainly is true that bond prices change daily—in fact, by the minute. And if interest rates rise by 3 or 4%, the price of bonds will plummet. That happened in 1994, for example. Bonds, along with mutual funds based on bonds and mortgages, took a nose-dive, and a lot of silly investors sold them in a panic, only to watch them all soar when rates eventually came back down.

But remember this key fact: You lose money when interest rates rise only if you sell the bond! Hang on to it until maturity and you get exactly what you always knew you'd get: face value.

Regardless of what rates do between now and 2002, I know exactly what my Ontario strip bond will dump into my RRSP, and that's $194,000.

But I don't think interest rates are going to rise much, if at all. Rather, I believe rates are in a long-term decline, along with inflation. That means odds are your strip bonds will rise in market value in the future, not fall.

In fact, a year after I bought that Ontario bond for $51.75 per $100, it was selling for $56.38, so I could unload the bond for $109,394, and take a $9,000 capital gain for holding the investment a year. Because interest rates had fallen, and the bond was a year closer to maturity, it had become more valuable.

Inside my RRSP, that would be realized free of tax, equal to a one-year, 9% return, several points higher than a GIC. Outside my RRSP, the money would be subject to capital gains tax of 36%, substantially less than the tax on GIC interest of 54%.

Here is an example of a strip bond hard at work, and giving me investment choices. I can simply hang on to it and double my money, or I can gamble that interest rates will fall and continue to rack up capital gains. Even if I lose that gamble, rates rise and my gain is wiped out, I know I will always have $194,000 paid to me by the Province of Ontario on maturity day. How can I lose? Just one way—panicking if rates do surge, and selling the bond.

Government bonds come in maturities ranging from 6 months to 30 years. Shorter-term, mini-bonds are called Treasury bills (T-bills), also backed by the power to tax and available in terms of 30, 60, 90 or 180 days. They're a good place to park cash for a while.

Strip bonds exist in various forms—a step-up bond offers escalating annual rates, and a callable bond can be redeemed by the lender at certain times prior to maturity. Some investment firms will "package" together a number of bonds of various types and maturities specifically for RRSPs. Many of these offerings are excellent, and just having access to them alone is worth the effort in finding a good, independent financial adviser.

But you can also buy bonds at the bank. Currently the Toronto-Dominion is the only one selling strip bonds directly to the public at the branch level. But the bank is not in the business of giving detailed financial advice, so there are still advantages to doing your bond-buying through your personal adviser.

Now, strip bonds are wonderful RRSP instruments, and every portfolio should have some. But make sure your asset mix is right—and that bonds (fixed income) are held alongside equities and mutual funds (growth assets).

Outside an RRSP, strips are less attractive, because Revenue Canada will tax you on interest income you have not yet received. That's the same negative tax situation as a GIC—so both should properly be tax-sheltered. Outside the RRSP it makes more sense to be putting your money into mutual funds, which are taxed only when they give you capital gains—and at a lower rate.

STRIPS VERSUS GICS: THE SCORECARD

Strip bonds	GICs
Yield 7% to 8%	Yield 6% (1997 rates)
1 to 30 years	5 years
Cashable anytime	Locked in
Rise when rates fall (capital gain potential)	No fluctuation
Unlimited government guarantee	$60,000 deposit-insurance limit
Buy at discount to face value	Interest paid on maturity
Taxable yearly (except if in RRSP)	Taxable yearly (except if in RRSP)

Building a maturity ladder

Here's a risk-free, long-term investment and retirement strategy you just can't beat. Because strip bonds are purchased at a discount to face value, the longer until a bond matures, the cheaper it is to buy now.

Here's an example: When my mother was 81 (I am forbidden to reveal her current age), she wanted to leave some money for educating a grandchild—money that wouldn't be needed for 15 years. She could have set aside $8,000 from her estate to be paid to the kid or, better idea, she could spend the money sending herself on a cruise and use just a fraction more to buy a strip bond that would accomplish the same purpose.

So she did.

She bought a strip maturing in 2010, which would be worth $8,000. For each $100 of the bond, she paid just $24.88, so the total cost of buying the bond was $1,999. And the interest that will end up in the hands of the grandchild is $6,000, plus the bond purchase price.

Now, isn't this a ducky thing to do if you are, say, a 47-year-old Baby Boomer like me—somebody who is 22 years from having to convert his RRSP into a RRIF?

You bet it is. In fact, every Boomer should be doing exactly this, assembling a ladder of strip bonds with staggered maturity dates to ensure a cash stream in the future. As each strip bond matures, the money can be spent on more strips to keep the ladder going. Once in place, the effect of compounding interest is awesome.

Imagine if you expanded on what my mother did. If, for the next 15 years, you put your annual RRSP contribution into a strip bond with a 15-year maturity, then every year, starting in 2012 and lasting until 2027, you'd have money coming due as retirement income.

How much?

That depends on the future direction of interest rates. But if we used my mother's example, paying $24.88 for every $100 in maturity value, a $10,000 RRSP contribution made today will ensure a return of $40,192 in 15 years.

Yes, and that's guaranteed.

Or you can purchase a number of strip bonds with varying maturity dates, with money you may now have inside your RRSP, to get a maturity ladder in place right away.

So, Boomers now in their forties and fifties can plan for stable retirement income by purchasing strip bonds with maturities of 15, 20, or even 30 years. That will mean receiving between $4 and $6 in the future for every $1 invested now. Using a maturity ladder you can leverage each year's allowable RRSP contribution into one more year of financial security decades from now.

Why isn't everyone doing this?

They must be too busy worrying about the future.

GENERATIONAL STRATEGIES

> *The power of demographic forces is overwhelming, altering the social fabric of nations and driving the economic trends.*
>
> —*Dr. Sherry Cooper, Chief Economist, Nesbitt Burns*

Too many Canadians believe there is a one-kind-fits-all investment strategy for successful retirement planning. Usually it goes like this: Get married, buy a house, pay it off, invest in risk-free RRSP assets like bonds and GICs, sell the house for big bucks, move into a condo and spend six months of the year being irradiated in Arizona or Florida.

Unfortunately there are some giant flaws in that plan. Real assets like real estate have a limited future. The return on "safe" and traditional retirement assets like bonds and investment certificates is too low to keep pace with increased longevity. North America is trying to digest the world's biggest demographic bulge, which will distort financial markets for the next two decades. And, of course, your marriage has a fifty–fifty chance of dissolving, which means family retirement assets may be carved in half.

On top of that, the Canada Pension Plan is in deep trouble—no matter what tinkering is done to it—which means Baby Boomers may well never see a government cheque in old age. And people nearing retirement age today face the spectre of double taxation starting in 2001, when the Seniors Benefit kicks in.

And then there are the Gen Xers, likely destined to pay more in taxes for a less certain future than the self-absorbed, live-for-today Boomers who went before, and who were largely responsible for some $600 billion in public debt.

> *Now, don't get me wrong: I still believe despite all these obstacles that the future—the next decade and a half, at least—will be wonderful for those who adopt the right investment strategies.*

Financial markets will sparkle; the cost of living will stay low; technology will continue to create unheard-of new opportunities; interest rates will fall; Canada's political uncertainty will end; and your assets can double every 60 months without taking on more risk than, say, driving through Winnipeg.

But you've got to know what to do, and when to do it. Now, more than ever, investment strategies must be appropriate to your age. Here are my basic suggestions:

GENERATION XERS

You have not been dealt a fair hand, but you'll have to make the most of it. The Boomers will live longer than any generation before them, hanging on to their jobs as long as possible and costing a fortune in retirement benefits. Even if public pensions will not be there for them (a likely scenario), the health-care bill alone will be staggering.

That spells even higher taxes and, worse, a declining economy starting sometime after 2015. Things will get ugly for the same reason they are now streaking higher—demographics. Those same Boomers are entering their most productive years now, and the North American economy will be robust for years to come. But after that, with millions of 60-year-olds around, economic growth could flame out fast.

As American demographer Harry Dent has predicted, it could result in the "Mother of all depressions." Here's how he described it in his visionary 1993 book, *The Great Boom Ahead*:

"How long will the depression last? Twelve to 15 years. Why? The peak of baby boom births occurred between 1957 and 1961. The next wave of births did not turn up until 1973 to 1976, or 12 to 15 years later. So you can expect a major economic downturn starting around 2010 and lasting to 2022 to 2025. No amount of government stimulus will prevent it, just as it didn't prevent the Great Depression of the 1930s."

Cheery stuff, right? Let's hope Dent is wrong. But I suspect he isn't.

That means Gen Xers cannot afford to waste any time. You have to be aggressively investing now, and for the next 15 years, as there is a good chance you may face a depression, complete with sustained and widespread job losses, in the middle of your working life.

You must maximize your RRSPs, making use of this best-possible tax shelter. Catch up on missed contributions, even if you have to borrow all the money—it still makes sense with today's low loan rates and the tax refund you'll receive. Make the overcontribution. Start income-splitting with your spouse as a long-term hedge against job loss. Use regular contributions to lower the tax bite on your paycheque.

Your RRSP assets should be 100% invested in high-growth investments—equities and equity-based mutual funds. When the market corrects, just step up your investment pace. The Dow Industrials and the TSE 300 are going to 8,000 or 9,000 over the next five to seven years—this is your best chance to build significant wealth, and quickly, in order to finance what could be a difficult second half of your life.

Be aggressive, and recognize the obvious opportunities at hand. The Internet is revolutionizing communications, and has only just begun to impact on consumers. So technology stocks will explode further in value. Then, an aging population will require far more health care than the public system can deliver. Wise investors will put money into nursing- and retirement-home companies, medical-care providers, biotechnology firms and health-care venture capitalists like the Canadian Medical Discoveries Fund.

Adopt a sensible real-estate strategy. It is now an excellent time to be a first-time home buyer with cheap mortgage rates, an abundant supply, reasonable prices and favourable government programs—so, go ahead, buy. That will stabilize your housing costs and allow you to build up other financial assets more quickly. Later on it will give you some equity to draw down.

But always be careful. The residential real-estate market could be collapsed within 15 years. Don't get caught. Buy a house you can see yourself living in for a long time.

BABY BOOMERS

The big generation also has some big problems, and huge chances to accumulate serious wealth. But as a generation, it's in terrible shape, having saved just about 5% of what will be needed to finance retirement within 20 years.

Too few Boomers appreciate what is happening to them, and the economic future. Within 35 years—when the average Baby Boomer

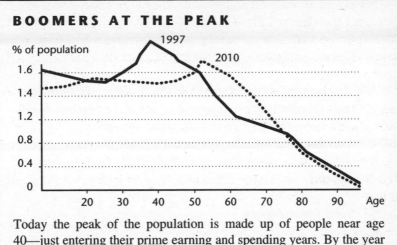

BOOMERS AT THE PEAK

Today the peak of the population is made up of people near age 40—just entering their prime earning and spending years. By the year 2010, they will be coming out of that period. Between now and then, close to 100 million middle-aged people will help sustain a strong North American economy.

Source: Canadian Institute of Actuaries

is 75, the number of retired people will have surged 142% while the Canadian population as a whole will have grown just 15%. By 2015, for the first time in history half the population will be over 40. By 2041—when the average Boomer is in his or her mid-eighties—the number of people the same age will have mushroomed 500%.

Just imagine the pressures that will be put on the economy having millions of new seniors. And health care? As Barbara Beck, of *The Economist*, has pointed out, "90% of the cost of medical care people consume over their lifetime is incurred in the six months before their death."

If this is depressing you, good. That's the point. Demographics are no longer on the side of the Baby Boomers. Our numbers will overwhelm the pension system and bankrupt public health care. If you want a happy and prosperous retirement, then you will have to earn it. Do not expect a dollar in government pensions. And expect to pay a substantial amount for adequate medical care.

> *Do not assume the treatment today's seniors receive—pension cheques and income supplements, free medical care and drugs, cheap nursing-home rates—will be there for retired Baby Boomers. You better expect to be on your own financially.*

This reality dictates an aggressive investment and tax strategy for the next 15 or 20 years. There is still time. You can do it even if you are 45 and have saved nothing. Using the RRSP actions I have outlined, there is no reason to fear what's coming. You can be ready.

- *You cannot afford to miss a single RRSP contribution.*
- *You cannot afford to invest in a GIC or savings bond.*
- *You have to raise your tolerance for risk.*
- *You must reconsider your real-estate assets.*
- *You must reduce your tax profile by every means possible.*
- *You must achieve double-digit rates of return on your investments.*

Finally.

Source: *Today's Seniors*

Baby boomers hit mid-life crisis

ing drop in the marriage rate, as   and founded Environics while a
couples chose to live together   graduate student at the Univer-

The baby boom

Source: *The Toronto Star*

Fortunately for all Baby Boomers, there is salvation at hand. You can dodge the demographic bullet, due to the incredible convergence of low inflation, falling rates and rising financial markets. This is a historic opportunity to grow your wealth. The great second chance is here. Don't blow it.

Baby Boomers can no longer afford to be savers. They have to be investors. Savers put money into guaranteed investment certificates, Canada Savings Bonds, money-market mutual funds, treasury bills and bank deposits.

But interest rates are low, and probably going lower over the next decade. The return Boomers need is simply not there. You will have to invest more aggressively in the stock and bond markets and in mutual funds, especially equity funds, which reflect market performance around the world. Sure, there is more risk and volatility involved here. But buy and hold quality investments; ride out the market fluctuations; and a decade from now I am certain you will have grown your wealth in a way not possible with low-risk, fixed-term assets.

Catch up on missed RRSP contributions, including the $2,000 overcontribution. And do it now. With a mountain of unused-contribution room building up, Ottawa is likely to cut off the ability to do this, because it poses a massive potential tax loss. Borrow to do this if you have to.

Use self-directed RRSPs to give yourself maximum investment flexibility. Don't be talked into a GIC-type RRSP at the bank or trust company. Don't be scared off, thinking you will have to manage this yourself. And do not be deterred by the non-tax-deductible fees. This is

The continent's top Boomer turned 50 last summer. Every seven seconds for the next 10 years somebody in North America will join him.

Source: *The Toronto Star*

money well spent to allow your plan to move assets where they can achieve the greatest return.

Invest for growth. Baby Boomers need to be at least 75% invested in stocks or equity-based mutual funds. The less you have accumulated so far, the more aggressive the funds should be. Remember: You need double-digit rates of return to grow the average Boomer RRSP of around $30,000 into at least $500,000 a decade and a half from now.

If you can't sleep at night with all your money in volatile funds, if you need some fixed-income, then **find better alternatives to your GICs.** Wait until they mature, cash them in, and invest in government strip bonds. You will get a greater rate of return, the potential of a capital gain if interest rates fall, and more security because there's no limit to the amount the government will guarantee. They're also fully cashable at any time.

Get liquid. **Start cashing out your real-estate equity.** For many Boomers this will be the hardest step emotionally, because we matured in an era when real estate equated with wealth, when a house was an inflation hedge providing a tax-free capital gain.

But those days are over. The trend now is away from real assets and to financial ones as low inflation rates make money more valuable. In the future it will be harder to sell your home, and the real-estate market may not come back in any real way for more than 20 years. It will never in your lifetime come back to resemble 1980 boom conditions. So the best thing you can do is unlock the equity in your home, which is now likely earning a zero rate of return, and get it into growth funds. You can do this by selling and downsizing in the kind of real estate that does have a future, or by taking a home-equity loan and creating a tax deduction at the same time.

Get professional financial help. The greatest mistake most people make is thinking they can figure all this out for themselves. Most can't. Most fail. Most believe that working with a financial adviser will cost them a lot of money or soak them in commissions. Those are dangerous myths. They will result in impoverished years in retirement for Boomers who try to ape their parents' strategy of buying a house, paying it off, working like hell and hoping for the best.

That worked when we had inflation and an expanding tax base. It doesn't work today. I would not dream of managing my own portfolio, despite all the time I have put into this area. I also wouldn't try to fix the hard drive on my computer or the timing on my car. So why would I try to pick the best nine mutual funds out of a thousand?

Hedge against the loonie. That's right—*je me souviens*. The premier of Quebec is a separatist and he says there will be another referendum on sovereignty. In fact he says there will be referendums until a majority of Quebeckers support breaking away from Canada.

Whatever your political hue, this much is certain: Financial markets hate uncertainty, and the dollar is at risk so long as the threat of a referendum is in the air. It is simply prudent not to have all your wealth in Canadian dollars if you are more than a decade away from retirement. That means international mutual funds, foreign-denominated bonds, foreign-currency dividend income and a lot of other smart, Bouchard-proofed investments. I bet he's got some.

JUNIOR SENIORS

Lots of people aged 55 to 75 make the same mistake, thinking they are at a stage in life where they can afford to take no risks with their investments and must be satisfied with nothing more than pension and interest income. Wrong—in fact, dangerous.

First, you will pay the most tax on pension and interest payments and, with the double taxation of the Seniors Benefit coming in 2001, anyone approaching 65 has to seriously reassess his or her financial strategy.

Second, people in their sixties often fail to budget enough for the future. After all, you stand a very good chance of living another 20 years, and the greatest risk is running out of money before you run out of life. In addition, the last years of your life can often be the most expensive, requiring extensive medical care or special housing.

Third, interest rates are on the decline, so maturing fixed-income investments like GICs will only offer you less income in the future, not more. It's time you cashed them in and found something better.

Replace maturing GICs with bonds or other superior investments like mortgage-backed securities. You will earn a greater return with less risk. You'll also get more flexibility and the potential for a capital gain. And when your GICs mature, view it as an opportunity to get some of that capital invested for far greater returns, because …

You should be 50% invested for growth. That means quality stocks and quality equity-based mutual funds. Break the interest-only mentality that keeps seniors' incomes far lower than they need to be. Participate in rising financial markets, higher corporate profits and expanding economies around the world. You have years and years yet to finance, and to enjoy.

Use a systematic withdrawal plan for income. This is a way of taking money out of a mutual fund on a regular basis, paying substantially less tax than you would getting an income stream from a GIC or a pension. Why? Because the fund pays you capital gains, which are taxed at a far lower rate. And the long-term performance is far superior to any return you can get on fixed-income. A $100,000 investment in Trimark's Canadian-dollar fund in 1981 would have given you a $10,000 annual income, and be worth about $500,000 today. Or $100,000 invested in Fidelity Growth America in 1990 would have paid the same, and today be worth almost $300,000.

All the quality mutual-fund companies—Templeton, C.I., Mackenzie, Dynamic, AGF, G.T., BPI, Investors and others—offer withdrawal plans that your financial adviser can tailor to meet your long-term income needs. For heaven's sake, do not rely on the teller at the corner bank to give you advice.

Don't sit on real-estate equity. Why would you have tens of thousands of dollars in real estate, earning you nothing, when that money could be yielding you income—financing travel, building an estate for your children, or just giving you a superior quality of life? It's time to sell, and downsize. Or to move into a rented condo. At this age real estate can turn into a trap—expensive to maintain and to insure.

If you are over age 50, you seriously have to question how much of your wealth you can afford to keep in a non-performing asset like your home. If you hang on to it for another 10 years, who will be the buyer?

Do sensible estate planning. If you do not plan properly, your estate will be decimated by taxes. Your wishes may not be carried out if you lack the proper documentation. If you die with real estate, it may saddle your children with a huge tax liability. How about probate fees and power of attorney? Have you named beneficiaries for your RRSPs? Have you estimated what your terminal tax return might look like? Do you have a will and an executor?

Dying is a complicated process. You've got to be ready. And ignoring the consequences can mean real financial hardship for those you leave behind. For a comprehensive overview of estate planning, you can read Sandra Foster's new book, *You Can't Take It with You*, published by John Wiley. And, of course, you must work on the plan with your financial adviser, then keep it current.

SENIOR SENIORS

Yes, things finally start to get simpler when you are 75 or older. But with longevity on the rise, people in this age bracket still have a lot of life left. As mentioned already, these can in fact be some of the most expensive years, as well.

Bear these points in mind:

Ditch the GICs, and be liquid. There is simply no reason to be locking up money for five-year periods just to get a return of less than 10%. The yield will be far higher from a government bond (not a savings bond), and you will still have liquidity—the ability to cash it in at any time if your circumstances change.

Maintain a growth component to your portfolio. Seniors at this age should still have at least 25% of their assets invested in equity-based mutual funds or quality stocks giving them dividend income. The growth will help finance the next decade, and the tax implications are far more favourable than interest income.

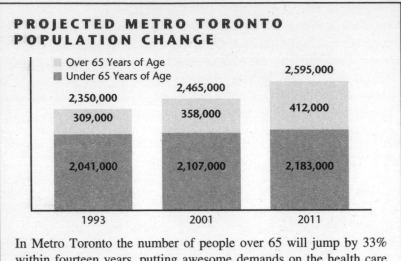

PROJECTED METRO TORONTO POPULATION CHANGE

- Over 65 Years of Age
- Under 65 Years of Age

	1993	2001	2011
Total	2,350,000	2,465,000	2,595,000
Over 65	309,000	358,000	412,000
Under 65	2,041,000	2,107,000	2,183,000

In Metro Toronto the number of people over 65 will jump by 33% within fourteen years, putting awesome demands on the health care system. Expect more fee-for-service and privatization. Another reason seniors need growth investment.

Source: Ontario Ministry of Finance

As should junior seniors, you should be using a systematic withdrawal plan to get regular income from these mutual funds.

Sell your real estate immediately. There is simply no solid financial reason not to. The capital could be out earning a lot more in the economy than in your house. The real-estate market is currently more buoyant than it's been in some time, and you might get a better price today than in a year or two. The house is costly to keep, and there is no shortage of quality retirement housing coming onstream in virtually every major centre in the country. It's time you moved.

Get a financial adviser you trust. You need to have an effective estate plan, along with proper tax planning and investment strategies. If you have not worked with an adviser in the past, this is a good time to start, considering the implications of not having in place things like a proper power of attorney.

Finally …

Go for a cruise. This is what it's all about—financial security so you can make the most of life! Money is not an object in itself, just a tool to help you accomplish other things. Lots of seniors worry about having enough, without ever enjoying what they have. Enough already. Lighten up!

Chapter 6

How to Find an Adviser You Can Trust

Most Canadians are gambling horribly with their financial futures and they don't even know it. Why? Because they entrust their money entirely to rank amateurs with no formal training who devote, on average, about two hours a year to the job and refuse to consider any research or investment information that isn't free. That's right—they try to do their own financial planning. Big, big mistake.

Need evidence?

- **Record numbers of people in 1995 and 1996 went bankrupt**, just as interest rates and unemployment were declining, the country was doing record amounts of trade, and corporate profits were at all-time high levels.

- Canadians continue to have about 70% of their net worth locked up in one type of asset that has been declining in value for most of the decade—**residential real estate**. That makes us some of the least diversified investors on the planet. Most people think real estate moves in cycles and all the equity they have lost in their homes will return. Sure, along with Elvis.

- **About two-thirds of Canadians have never made an RRSP contribution**, despite the fact this is the continent's best tax shelter. And most taxpayers have no idea that with one phone call they can open an RRSP with no cash and transfer into it things they already own, earning a rebate cheque from the government.

- Dan Richards, of Toronto-based Marketing Solutions, does public surveys showing **Canadians know next to nothing about investing**.

Canadians raid RRSP nest eggs

Record numbers need cash now, StatsCan says

By Tim Harper
OTTAWA BUREAU

OTTAWA — Canadians are dipping into retirement nest

much as possible, and obviously, we've got to monitor the situation.

"The CPP is a joint (federal-provincial) responsibility. We've had one meeting. We'll be meeting in the not-too-distant future on that."

StatsCan analyst Hubert Frenken said the move to get

Not a good sign. Half the number of people currently cashing in their RRSPs are under the age of 45.

Source: *The Toronto Star*

For example, most people think Canada Savings Bonds provide an excellent long-term return, when they actually wither as an investment. And only a quarter of people with bond or mortgage mutual funds know those funds will fall when interest rates rise. And, worse still, only 14% of people can identify the best-performing investment class since the Second World War. Of course: stocks.

• **Crazed investors sold hundreds of millions of dollars' worth of mutual funds** in the last three trading days before the Quebec referendum of October 30, 1995—just after the TSE 300 had been clobbered and those funds reduced in value. The day after the referendum, most of those people bought the funds back—at higher prices. So here's the traditional Canadian investment strategy: Sell low and buy high.

• People clamour to **buy investments when they are at their highest value and dump them when they fall**. Remember the folks lined up on Yonge Street in Toronto to buy gold at $1,000 an ounce? Today the metal is worth half of that, and no lineups. How about the people who bought houses at $1 million each on a nice street north of Toronto in 1989? Today half that street's for sale at $500,000 a house. And recall how many investors bailed out of their stocks after Black Monday, 1987? They missed one of the greatest run-ups in stock-market history.

Household debt reaching historic high

Canadians find themselves squeezed between out-of-control mortgages and maxed-out credit cards

| CANADIANS just can't stop spending. Buffeted by the recession. | **Cover Story** By Alanna Mitchell | uty chief economist at the Bank of Nova Scotia. He points out that households were carrying just $138-billion in | fallen, not risen. Pay raises? Try a few years of pay declines. And the security that owning a home was supposed to | pening three years after the previous recession, in a period of relatively strong economic growth. |

A decade ago household debt stood at 55% of income. Today it's at 88%. The savings rate is at a 24-year low.

Source: *The Globe and Mail*

- And surveys also show us that Canadians, on average, hold their mutual funds for about **18 months—a period of time so short it just about guarantees they will lose money**. This is especially true for people who invest in the no-load funds. Some are so obsessed with saving a few dollars that they trade off solid investment advice for no commission.

- Millions of Canadians keep **billions in low-yield guaranteed investment certificates** when they could be earning more of a return with less risk in other securities. Why? Because they've never heard of strip bonds or mortgage-backed securities.

I could go on for pages, but I hope this is enough for you to get my point: The average Canadian is the last person he or she should trust with something so important as personal financial planning, tax and investment strategies. And yet most do. It's sad. That's one reason a giant retirement crisis is going to descend on this country. It's why millions of Boomers will end up being both old and poor.

I've written before about my experiences giving financial seminars across Canada. Various companies hire me to give these, from the largest of Toronto-based national investment houses owned by the great banks, to individual financial planners in rural Nova Scotia and the Lower Mainland of British Columbia.

Invariably, the same pattern emerges: A few hundred people show up, and many of them are armed with notebooks and tape recorders. They madly scribble information for an hour and a half, and try to run for the door at the end of the evening before any representative of the hosting company can convince them to come in for a free consultation. At first I just thought they were being cheap—taking only what was offered for nothing. Then I realized most of them are just scared—worried about their own financial futures, but also convinced a financial planner will cost them a lot in commissions, and maybe lose their money in an investment they don't understand.

The irony is those people who do listen, and then take up the offer of professional money management, almost always go on to improve their wealth. By sharing the burden, they gain a lot.

Yes, there are rip-off artists

For the record, there have been a lot of people ripped off by unscrupulous financial advisers. Some advisers turn out to be nothing but churners— excessively buying and selling investments just to maximize commissions, at the expense of the client's portfolio.

Some of the "top producers" at rapidly growing financial-services companies get to be top producers not by making wise investments, but rather by racing through legions of clients.

Others are more motivated by the goodies flowing from mutual-fund companies than the best interests of investors. Ontario is one jurisdiction that is taking some action to curb that, backed by the Investment Funds Institute of Canada.

So you are right to approach this exercise with caution and care. But not with cynicism or as a sceptic. The simple truth is you will be better off with a personal financial adviser than trying to get all of your financial information at the corner bank (where you will be offered only the bank's own, limited products) from free seminars, the media or even incredibly wise books.

Here are my answers to the questions I'm most often asked about finding an adviser you can trust:

Advice on advisers—at a glance

How do I know if a planner is qualified? Are there regulations?
People who sell you financial securities have to be licensed. But the industry, as a whole, is unregulated, which means finding a good adviser is going to take some work on your part. The Canadian Association of Financial Planners has about 1,600 members, but that accounts for just 20% or so of all those people who call themselves planners.There are currently no national standards, but there are a few designations you should be aware of.

"Registered Financial Planner," or RFP, is a designation given by the Canadian Association of Financial Planners; "Chartered Financial Planner," or CFP, designates someone who's completed the correspondence course of the Canadian Institute of Financial Planning; and "Chartered Financial Consultant," or CFC, is an approval from the Life Underwriters of Canada.

To further confuse things, the Canadian Association of Financial Planners and the Life Underwriters have teamed up to create the Financial Planners Standards Council of Canada, which will be promoting yet another designation, "Certified Financial Planner," or, another CFP. It looks like this last one may turn out to be the industry norm, since that term is already recognized in the United States and a few other countries.

The bottom line is that you should make sure what training and education a planner has, along with experience and references.

What is this going to cost me?

Most people think a financial planner will cost them a huge amount of money. Usually, that's not the case. In fact, most planners work for you for free.

The right way to think about most planners is the same way you think about travel agents: You can get your ticket to Montreal and pay Air Canada $500, or your travel agent can arrange it for you, and it still costs $500.

That's because Air Canada will do a lot more business each year with your agent than with you, and so the airline is happy to pay the agent a commission—in effect, lowering the cost of the ticket.

So, your financial planner is paid a commission by the mutual-fund company or bond issuer when you add that investment to your portfolio. Of course, you can hire an adviser who is fee-only and does not actually arrange for any investments to be made. That will cost you up to $2,000 for a complete financial plan, and an hourly consultation fee ranging from $50 to $250, with most in the $100 area.

> *You will often see "expert" opinion in the media warning you away from commission-paid advisers and into the arms of fee-paid ones. Ignore it. For the vast majority of people who have under $1 million in liquid assets, an adviser who is remunerated through commissions is just fine.*

What can you expect from a person like that? For starters, a free first consultation, which will last an hour or 90 minutes. That will be followed by an analysis of your existing assets, and a draft financial plan, making recommendations. All of that typically costs you nothing—so what possible excuse could you have for not getting such a valuable second opinion on how you're doing?

Eight Common Investor Mistakes an Adviser Can Help You Avoid

- **Waiting for the "best" time to invest, or never investing**
- **Buying at a high price; selling at a low one**
- **Buying yesterday's hot investment**
- **Choosing investments not suited to individual goals or time horizons**
- **Failing to diversify; "putting all your eggs in one basket"**
- **Reacting to short-term events rather than long-term trends**
- **Basing investment decisions on fees and sales charges**
- **Basing investment decisions on emotions rather than facts**

Source: Mutual Fund Forum

Where do I start?

- You can ask others who they use as advisers, or family members, co-workers or the boss. Word-of-mouth references are good because you can get a feel for an adviser's track record from somebody you know.

- Naturally, you can respond to ads published in the financial section of your local newspaper, or in *The Financial Post*—especially during RRSP season, there are lots of them offering particular investments.

- Better still, go to a few financial seminars. Most of them are free and, again, during RRSP season, there is a flurry to choose from. A great deal of information can be had in a short period of time, and the financial planners hosting them invariably offer anyone who attends a free consultation in their office or home. This gives you an opportunity to meet, and assess, that person.

But a word of caution: Not all seminars are what they appear. Some are come-ons for expensive and needless courses on no-money-down real estate or sure-thing business opportunities. So, if you go, leave your chequebook at home.

Just listen and you can quickly determine if this is a shameless sales pitch—with one or two specific investment products being hyped—or the introduction to a service that might be useful and an adviser who sounds promising.

What questions should I ask?
When you have that first meeting, the adviser will ask for a lot of information on your income, assets, taxes, family situation and goals.

In return, you should ask about how that person expects to be paid, what areas of personal expertise he or she has; and what track record and credentials. Be tough. Be frank. Be candid. Ask where the adviser puts his or her own money, why and what the results have been.

Writing in *The Financial Post*, retired adviser Don Pooley, of Vancouver, suggested you should ask a potential adviser how old he or she is—because you may feel more comfortable with somebody of your own generation. Pooley also suggests asking of that person if he or she has professional liability insurance, such as errors-and-omissions insurance. That will protect you if something goes wrong, and is a sign "of prudence, an important trait in any financial planner."

Here is a list of questions American investors are urged to ask of a potential planner, published in *The Wall Street Journal* in recent months. It's a good one to start with:

Things You Should Ask Advisers During Interviews

- **What is your area of expertise?**

- **What is your approach to saving and investing?**

- **Will you provide an individualized financial plan?**

- **What kinds of communications can I expect from you on an ongoing basis (account statements, newsletters, etc.)?**

- **How often will you review my portfolio?**

- **How are you compensated for the service you provide?**

- **How are fees calculated?**

- **On average, how much can I expect to pay for your service?**

- **What do I receive in return for that fee?**

- **What, if anything, do you expect of me during our relationship?**

Should I ask for references?
Absolutely. This is the most important thing you should ask for. A good adviser has nothing to hide. In fact, a good adviser should have a lot to be proud of, and will want to share his or her clients' success with you.

So ask for a list of 10 or 12 people he or she has worked with. Then call and ask for a candid appraisal of the planner's effectiveness. Has the adviser reduced their tax bill? Increased their net worth? Diversified their investments? What overall rate of return are they getting on their portfolios? How often do they hear from the adviser? Are they kept fully informed? Are they concerned about excessive trading in their accounts? Are they related to the adviser? (It does happen!)

What level of service should I expect?

Several meetings at first to approve an investment and tax strategy, then regular updates—perhaps quarterly. Your portfolio should be reviewed several times a year, or as changing conditions dictate.

You should get a regular account statement—monthly is best—and that statement should break down all transactions, giving you rates of return and securities held along with weightings by asset class (for example, 41% mutual funds, 32% fixed income, 27% equities).

Many good advisers provide clients with newsletters; access to investment research; or client-appreciation nights, where investment professionals come to speak. Advisers with some of the larger investment firms (Nesbitt Burns, Wood Gundy, RBC Dominion Securities, ScotiaMcLeod, Midland Walwyn and Richardson Greenshields, T-D Evergreen, Yorkton Securities) also are backed by substantial research departments, along with access to new stock and bond offerings.

The most important thing to expect is a comfortable working relationship with somebody you trust.

How can I tell if it's not working?

A tell-tale sign you're working with the wrong person is churning. That's when the adviser is buying and selling a lot of mutual-fund units or stocks for no good reason other than to earn more in commission. Check your regular statement and look for any evidence of unnecessary trades.

What's the difference between a planner, a broker and a counsellor?

As mentioned above, anybody can call him- or herself a **financial planner**, and there are no national standards or regulations. But that does not mean you should look elsewhere. Far from it—using a planner whom you get along with can be the most cost-effective way of building wealth.

Many planners work for companies that offer a full range of financial products, including strip bonds, stocks, mutual funds, GICs and more. Examples of these are the Financial Concept Group, The Financial Planning Group, DPM Financial Planning, Partners in Planning, Money Concepts, Regal Capital, Capital Management Group and Fortune Financial. Investors Group is the largest in terms of assets managed and has recently moved far beyond its own range of mutual funds to offer clients dozens more.

The planners with these companies usually earn their living through commissions paid by the mutual fund and other companies. Ask, and most are happy to tell you exactly who pays them, and how much.

A **broker** is licensed to sell any financial product and must have completed the Canadian Securities Course. He or she will work for a brokerage company regulated by the Investment Dealers Association of Canada. A broker will also earn money through commissions on every transaction in your account.

An investment **counsellor** is paid through fees, which can take the form of an annual payment or a percentage of the total portfolio under management. Usually counsellors are the preserve of the rich—those with more than $500,000 in investible assets. They, by the way, account for only 1.6% of the population. Pity.

How do I know if an adviser is full-service?

Ask. Some planners only sell mutual funds, so obviously they will not be able to give your portfolio the balance and diversity it should have. Everybody needs a little fixed-income, for example, and you also want an adviser who will look at your total financial picture—real estate, insurance, estate, tax and investment plans.

Remember the people at the bank or trust company will offer you only the products that institution itself sells (with the exception of Toronto-Dominion, which is slowly offering more and more competitors' mutual funds). In my opinion, you will almost always be best helped by a full-service independent financial advisory company or a broker

What about the discount brokers?

These are no-frills operations that allow you to buy stocks, bonds or funds at a vastly cheaper commission cost than with a full-service broker or planner. Examples are T-D's impressive Green Line operation and the Royal Bank's Action Direct.

The discount brokers are innovative and cutting-edge in terms of the latest investor technology. Canada Trust, Action Direct and Green

Line all offer the option of real-time trading via personal computer and modem—an experience that can get any living person's adrenaline coursing.

The down-side is the same as with no-load mutual funds, which is, no-help. The people on the other end of the phone or the modem line are order-takers, not experienced investment advisers.

The discounters also don't publish research, send out in-depth newsletters or call you with new initial public offerings (IPOs). But if you know what you want to buy, and are determined to save some dollars on commission—accepting the risk of a bad decision—then go for it.

Should I go with a small company or a big one?

There is no right answer to this question, because it is the individual adviser that really matters. The advantage of a small office or firm is that you stand a better chance of getting personal service from an experienced individual.

But the advantage of a large firm is access to research and, of course, a full range of investment options. I have dealt with scores of advisers, brokers and their support staff across the country, and my personal recommendation would be to find a small office of a big company. That way you can establish a close relationship with the people working there, and still enjoy the benefits accorded the clients of the busiest downtown mega-operation.

And always remember this: A good financial adviser is more interested in a long-term relationship with you than in making quick commissions. As your wealth grows, so does the adviser's compensation—so over a 15- or 20-year time line, your financial well-being is your adviser's main concern. Put yourself in his or her chair, and you realize quickly this is the prudent way to build a business.

So, if you're getting churned, you're getting burned. Move on.

Should I give over all my money?

Probably not—at least not at first. You need to build a relationship and also see the wisdom of your adviser at work. So, don't write a cheque representing your life savings right off the bat. But, by the same token, don't hand over $5,000 and expect to see dramatic results in a few weeks

Once you feel comfortable with the advice you are getting, it does make sense to consolidate your portfolio with one person. That way you can achieve diversity; organize the best tax-planning strategies; and ensure the right mix of mutual funds, bonds, real estate and equities for your stage of life and risk tolerance.

Where do I go from here?

Why not come out to a financial seminar and meet some planners? Make up your own mind.

My current seminar schedule is available through my Internet website. Here's how to reach me:

- By phone: (416) 489-2188

- By fax: (416) 489-2189

- By e-mail: garth@garth.ca

- On the World Wide Web: http://www.garth.ca

- By lettermail: Garth Turner, Suite 310, 1670 Bayview Ave., Toronto, M4G 3C1

- Through my agent: David Lavin Agency
  24 Duncan Street, 4th Floor, Toronto, M5V 2B8
  1-800-265-4870; (416) 979-7979
  Fax: (416) 979-7987

Internet Resources

You can use the Internet to shop for a financial planner, buy mutual-fund units, get free financial advice and access the brightest minds at the country's top accounting and pension consultancy firms. The amount of information is daunting. No, it is overwhelming. You can drown in the stuff.

Besides, it changes by the hour, with new websites being created and loaded up with material. I have no doubt that, by the time these words are printed and in your hands, there will be more excellent offerings on the World Wide Web and other areas of the Internet. All you have to do is a net-search using the word "investment" or "retirement" and hundreds of entries will appear before you.

If you do not have a computer or access to the Internet, don't worry: Simply finding a good financial adviser is all the help 99% of Canadians need. But if you do, and are willing to devote a few hours to comparing sites, here are some to check out. Several of these you will find linked to my own website, along with banks, government resources, economics departments, news organizations and others.

My website address is http://www.garth.ca.

FINANCIAL ADVISERS

Regional contact names and phone numbers for the Canadian Association of Financial Planners are listed on one website, which also has areas explaining the basics of financial planning, and even offers answers to your questions by e-mail. It also has a good checklist on how to find a financial adviser, and planning tips.

Canadian Association of Financial Planners
http://www.cafp.ca

As well, The Fund Library's site, which is getting about 50,000 hits a day, has the online resumés of about a hundred investment advisers.

The Fund Library
http://www.fundlib.com/ibd

Financial planning software

A superior site for financial planning; mutual-fund information; and links to an astounding number of companies, resources and individual financial planners is the one run by The Fund Library. You can also join a discussion group on mutual-fund strategies. And it offers free financial-planning software, including Trimark's interactive educational program.

The Fund Library
http://www.fundlib.com/

Retirement planning

Many sites are available, and the two mentioned above have links to several of them. Perhaps the best is RetireWeb, which is packed with information and run by actuary Scott Parkinson, complete with separate areas for people retired, nearly retired or years from it. Access government programs from here, use the powerful calculators to determine retirement-income needs, or if you should be paying your mortgage off instead of making RRSP contributions. It does everything except tell you how long you'll live.

RetireWeb
http://www.retireweb.com

Tax planning

One good place to start is Revenue Canada's website, which offers instant online access to all those guides and brochures that can take forever to arrive by mail. It also lists the latest tax rulings and changes, along with RevCan initiatives that are useful to know about.

Revenue Canada
http://www.revcan.ca

Tax preparation

Although I think most people who prepare their own income-tax returns are either cheap or delusional, there's little doubt some good tax-return software will help cut down on the errors. Here are two to sample.

CanTax
http://www.cantax.com

TaxPrep
http://www.taxprep.com

Accounting firms

Believe it or not, but Canada's largest accounting firms are innovative, aggressive and incredibly useful sources of information on the Internet. They offer the best analysis of federal and provincial budgets, and even have interactive question-and-answer areas where you can access a tax professional. You can also download current tax tables and calculate your tax liability.

KPMG
http://www.kpmg.ca

Ernst & Young
http://www.inforamp.net/ey

Deloitte & Touche
http://ftn/DT/index-eng.html

Stock quotes

It is now possible to get real-time stock quotes, buy securities online and get instant access to high-quality and current charts and graphs of stock performance—once the stuff reserved for the eyes of stock-brokers only. Several of these sites also provide powerful calculators and links to major U.S. financial sites.

Quote.com
http://www.quote.com/

PAWWS Financial Network
http://www.pawws.secapl.com/

Security APL Quote Service
http://www.secapl.com/cgi-bin/qs

Stockmaster
http://www.stockmaster.com/

Canadian Stock Market Reporter
http://www.canstock.com

CT Securities International Inc.
http://www.ctsecurities.com

PC Quote In.
http://www.pcquote.com

NETWorth
http://www.networth.galt.com

Telescan
http://host.telescan.com

Security APL
http://www.secapl.com/cgi-bin/qs

InterQuote
http://www.interquote.com

Montreal Stock Exchange
http://www.me.com

Vancouver Stock Exchange
http://www.vse.com

Alberta Stock Exchange
http://www.alberta.net

Nasdaq Stock Market
http://www.nasdaq.com

American Stock Exchange
http://www.amex.com

Chicago Mercantile Exchange
http://www.cme.com

Holt's Market Report
http://207.67.198.21/holt/index.html

Stock trading

There are currently no Canadian investment firms who offer stock trading on the Internet, although as I write this, Toronto-Dominion Bank's innovative Green Line Investment Services is preparing to go online with such a service. But there are several ways to trade U.S. stocks, in what is a direct challenge to traditional stock exchanges. This is probably the least expensive way possible to execute a trade—as low as $14.95 U.S.

E*Trade Securities
http://www.etrade.com

E.Schwab Online Investing
http://www.schwab.com

Lombard Institutional Brokerage
http://www.lombard.com

Aufhauser & Co.
http://198.200.173.81

Stock information

The first and only real-time news release database is Canada Stockwatch, which provides all the news releases for all Canadian public companies. That means it has more than 400,000 releases, giving invaluable amounts of information on companies you might want to buy stocks in.

Canada Stockwatch
http://www.canada-stockwatch.com/

MarketEdge
http://www.marketedge.com

Investors Edge
http://www.irnet.com

StockSmart
http://www.stocksmart.com

Hoover's Handbook
http://www.hoover.com

Mutual funds

The fund companies have taken to the Net in a big way, and some of the sites are comprehensive—and getting a lot of traffic. Many of these offer daily news-briefing services; overviews of the equity and bond markets; fund quotes; links to American sites; performance graphs; economics reports; and much, much more. Of course, they contain extensive information on the various funds offered. It pays to surf before you buy.

One site bears special mention for its huge library of links to other financial sites, including all major mutual funds, search engines, news sources, stock and mutual-fund quotes, precious-metals websites and more—thanks to the Royal Bank.

Royal Mutual Funds
http://www.royalbank.com/english/fund

Here are the other major Canadian mutual fund locations, listed alphabetically (the prefix to all the addresses is http://www.).

Admax Regent
admaxregent.com

AGF Management
agf.com

Altamira
altamira.com

BMO First Canadian Fund
fcfunds.bomil.ca

CIBC Funds
cibc.com/inside/investment/mf.html

C.I. Mutual Funds
cifunds.com

Canada Trust
canadatrust.com/ct/mutual/index.html

Dynamic Mutual Funds
dynamic.ca

Elliot & Page
fundlib.com/ellpage.html

G.T. Global
gtglobal.ca

Investors Group
investorsgroup.com/funds

Mackenzie Financial
fundlib.com/mackenzie.html

Sagit Investment
direct.ca/funds/

Scotia Excelsior Funds
scotiabank.ca/nonreg.htm

Scudder Canada
scudder.ca

Talvest
talvest.com/homee.html

TD Mutual Funds
tdbank.ca/tdbank/mutual/index/html

Templeton Canada
templeton.ca

Trimark Investment Management
trimark.com

University Avenue
fundlib.com/univers.html

Investment advice, publications and newsletters

Here are some sites I have visited that offer reams of information on investment trends, high-tech stocks, financial gossip and insider reports, corporate profiles and more.

InvestLink
http://www.investlink.com

InvestorsEdge
http://www.irnet.com

The Newsletters Page
http://www.myna.com/~invest/p-nleter.htm

Wall Street Online
http://www.wso.com/wso/

The Newsletter Library
http://pub.savvy.com/

The Silicon Investor
http://www.techstocks.com

Barron's Magazine
http://www.barrons.com

Money Magazine
http://www.moneymag.com

Bloomberg Business News
http://www.bloomberg.com

Internet web-search engines

These are simply devices to help you find more related sites on the Internet. You can find search-engines in countless places on the World Wide Web, but three of the mains ones—Webcrawler, Yahoo and Lycos—are on the Investment Funds Institute of Canada site, along with links to mutual funds, industry information and a glossary of investment terms.

Investment Funds Institute of Canada
http://www.mutfunds.com/ific

St. Clair Financial Index
http://www.findex.com/search/htm

My belief is the Internet will become the primary source of financial information in the years to come. The day is already here when you can do all your banking and investing from a home computer. Just a couple of years ago no major Canadian financial institution was on the Internet—today they are competing vigorously in cyberspace.

For the average investor, this is incredibly empowering. We have access to more information than has ever been offered before. The trick is to wade through and find what is of true value. Just as it is over-whelming to walk through a large library, trying to comprehend what lies in each volume, so the Internet is of no use unless mapped, chart-ed and bookmarked.

If you come across websites and Internet addresses you feel could help other RRSP investors, then please let me know and I will endeav-our to get that information in next year's version of this guide.

The Turner Report

The amount Canadians are borrowing through credit cards, lines of credit, loans and mortgages has never been higher. Household debt is at an unprecedented level. The savings rate is at a 24-year low.

Bankruptcies set a record in 1995. Then another one in 1996. The amount we have been saving for retirement has been falling steadily since 1979. Last year we failed to contribute over 80% of what the RRSP rules allowed.

Most people don't have an RRSP. A majority of people have no company pension. The public pension plan is being changed, so we will contribute more to it and get less in return. Middle-class seniors will have at least half their income taxed away after changes in the year 2001.

Does this sound like a recipe for retirement disaster?

You bet it does. But if you follow at least some of the strategies in this book, you should be better off than most people—at least prepared for what now appears to be the inevitable: the economic bankrupting of the country by the what-me-worry? attitude of the grey-templed Baby Boomers.

But, as I have also shown, for those people who realize where we are right now in the economic cycle, who see the fundamental shift from real assets to financial assets and who understand the actions of the worried Boomers over the next decade and a half, this is a time of unbridled opportunity.

> **Mercedes-Benz sales set a record in Canada last year. So did BMW. Obviously a growing number of people have this figured out.**

- You can borrow $50,000 or $100,000 from your paid-up real estate with a phone call at an effective rate of less than 3%.

- You can invest to earn double-digit rates of return in any one of hundreds of quality mutual funds.

- You can double and triple your money without risk in government bonds.

- You can use the government's own RRSP rules to sell yourself assets that you already own, and get a tax break for doing it.

- You can invest in a mutual fund, have it pay the interest on money borrowed to make the investment, and then write that interest off your taxable income.

- You can invest in oil and gas interests that give you cash income and a capital gain, and it's all tax-deductible.

- You can use an RRSP to leverage up the down-payment on a first home with money from Ottawa.

- And you can get wise and reputable financial advice for free.

With these things possible, why are most middle-class Canadians slipping behind financially?

It can only be because they're not aware of what a powerful time we live in for increasing personal assets. Money is cheap. Financial markets are soaring. Inflation is down. And the surge into mutual funds, equities and government securities by millions of people after the millennium—the year 2000, now just a few dozen months away—will make those who see it coming, and take action, secure and comfortable.

Will you be one of them?

I hope so. I hope this little book helped guide you. I enjoyed writing it, and intend on issuing a new chapter to it every month.

AN AFFORDABLE NEWSLETTER OF TAX AND INVESTMENT STRATEGIES

Beginning in March 1997, *The Turner Report* will be published—a newsletter you can receive 10 times a year to build on the information in this book. Its intention will be clear: To present current strategies for reducing your tax exposure, and investment opportunities that make sense.

It will cover mutual funds, strip bonds, real estate, precious metals, stocks, oil and gas and any other aspect of personal finance that you need to know about. *The Turner Report* will not suffer the long lead times that books demand, nor will it be another Bay Street publication written by a committee.

Instead, it will be the living extension of this book and my financial guide for Baby Boomers, *2015: After the Boom.* It will be as timely and inexpensive as I can possibly make it. The cost will be even less for those who wish to subscribe by e-mail or fax. Of course, those Internet and fax subscribers will also receive their newsletters faster than will lettermail subscribers.

The cost will be less than $5 an issue. And I will send you the first issue as a gift for subscribing. If you are not satisfied, send it back for a full refund. There is no risk.

Of course, there are many good investment newsletters currently in existence—devoted to stock picking, mutual-fund selection, gold and silver, or commercial real estate. But if I thought any one of them was adequate for aggressive middle-class Canadians, aged 30 to 55, who are determined to succeed, then I would simply recommend it, instead of writing my own.

But to date I have found none that combines tax and investment strategies in the big-picture context of where the economy is headed or what the impact of demographics will be. Nobody seems to be talking about what people want to hear: How can I get ahead at a time when salaries are frozen, jobs are not secure and taxes are rising?

There are ways. Powerful ones. And now, more than ever, the difference between financial independence and dependence has come down to one thing, and one thing only: knowledge.

**Clip or photocopy this coupon, and mail it to me at
Suite 310, 1670 Bayview Ave., Toronto M4G 3C1**

Subscribe now, and get your first issue FREE

A special offer for charter subscribers: The March '97 issue will be sent to you without charge. Your subscription will start with the next issue. If you are not pleased, return it for a full refund.

❏ By Lettermail: $49 a year
❏ By Fax: $45 a year
❏ By E-mail: $40 a year

Name:_____

Address:_____ Apt.:_____

City:_____ Prov.:_____ Code:_____

Phone: Home (   )_____ Business (   )_____

Name:_____

❏ Enclosed is: My cheque payable to *The Turner Report*

❏ Bill my VISA # _ _ _ _ / _ _ _ _ / _ _ _ _ / _ _ _ _

❏ Bill my MasterCard # _ _ _ _ / _ _ _ _ / _ _ _ _ / _ _ _ _

Mail to: The Turner Report   Expiry ____/____
          310—1670 Bayview Ave.,
          Toronto M4G 3C1
          or Fax to: (416) 489-2189

Index

accounting firms, 182
Action Direct, 177
Admax Regent, 185
age credit, 86
AGF funds, 141, 166, 185
Altamira funds, 77, 141, 185
alternative minimum tax, 9, 106
American University, 152
annuities, 103, 116
Armstrong, Philip, 142
asset allocation, 110, 156
attribution rules, 86, 87
Auerbach, Alan, 33

Baby Boomers, 12, 19, 21, 24,
    33, 67, 72, 86, 105, 121, 157,
    160
balanced funds, 77
Bank Credit Analyst, 146
Bank of Montreal, 83, 140, 141
Bank of Nova Scotia, 9, 92
bankruptcy, 57, 151, 169
Beck, Barbara, 161
Begg, Ron, 149
beneficiary, 50, 103, 151
Black Monday, 72, 170
BMO First Canadian funds, 185

BMW, 190
Boeda, Paul, 24
bond funds, 111
book value, 82
Bouchard, Lucien, 48, 80, 82,
    140
BPI funds, 166
Bre-X, 133, 146
Brown, Robert, 125
Buchanan, Peter, 140
Business Week, 151

Canada Deposit Insurance
    Corporation, 73, 154
Canada Mortgage and Housing
    Corporation, 49, 91, 93
Canada Pension Plan, 16, 25, 36,
    38, 39, 122, 158
Canada Savings Bonds, 75, 92,
    98, 153, 163, 170
Canada Stockwatch, 184
Canada Trust, 76, 92, 177, 185
Canadian Association of
    Financial Planners, 24, 172,
    180
Canadian Institute of Actuaries,
    33, 35, 38, 161

Canadian Institute of Financial
   Planning, 172
Canadian Medical Discoveries
   Fund, 150, 160
Canadian Real Estate
   Association, 49, 95
Canadian Securities Course, 177
Capital Management Group, 177
capital gains, 21, 54, 74, 99, 148
Cartaway Resources, 147
C.D. Howe Institute, 33
Cestnick, Tim, 21, 22
CFTO-TV, 42, 43
Chinloy, Peter, 152
Choucha, Jean-Paul, 42
churning, 176
C.I. funds, 128, 141, 166, 185
CIBC funds, 185
CIBC Wood Gundy, 140, 176
clawback of pension benefits, 18
Cohen, Bruce, 127
company pension, 28
Confederation Life, 83, 150
Cooper, Sherry, 158
creditors, 150
CT funds, 141

Deloitte & Touche, 9, 112
demographics, 35, 68, 152
Dent, Harry, 159
Department of Finance, 17, 81
dependents, 50, 103
diversification, 144, 148
dividends, 21, 54, 148
divorce, 51, 52, 70, 89, 103
dollar, 80, 143, 154
double taxation, 116, 134, 165
Dow Industrials, 72, 84, 145, 160
DPM Financial Planning, 177
Drache, Arthur, 15

Dussault, Bernard, 32
Dynamic funds, 166, 185

early retirement, 10
earned income, 52, 53, 55
Echo Boomers, 86
The Economist, 161
Elliot & Page, 186
Environics, 142
equity, 68, 92
escalating GICs, 76
estate planning, 167
Export Development
   Corporation, 154
extendible GICs, 75

federal budget, 10
federal debt, 34, 56
federal deficit, 56, 80
Fidelity funds, 69, 128, 141, 166
financial adviser, 77, 122, 148,
   169, 172, 176
Financial Concept Group, 177
Financial Planners Standards
   Council, 173
The Financial Planning Group,
   177
financial planning software, 181
financial seminars, 171, 174
fixed income assets, 111
fixed income funds, 77
flat taxes, 58
Fortune Financial, 177
Fund Library, 181

GE Capital, 91, 93
Generation X, 33, 36, 68, 86,
   125, 158, 159
generational strategies, 158
gold, 170

government bonds, 113
Grantier, Bruce, 9
Green Line funds, 77, 177, 184
growth assets, 113
G.T. funds, 186
Guaranteed Income Supplement,
    10, 16, 134
guaranteed investment certifi-
    cates (GICs), 12, 43, 72, 74,
    84, 111, 144

Hamilton, Malcolm, 14, 17, 19
health care, 32, 34, 40, 161
Home Buyers' Plan, 48, 49, 88,
    94, 95, 136
home equity loan, 70, 92
House of Commons finance
    committee, 123
house price average, 12

immigration, 68
income splitting, 44, 49, 103
inflation, 20, 27, 74, 98, 110,
    129
inheritance, 22, 106
inheritor, 51
initial public offerings, 178
Institute for Research on Public
    Policy, 36, 37
interest rates, 27, 48, 74, 110,
    155, 157, 163
Internet resources, 180
Investment Dealers Association,
    177
Investment Funds Institute, 177,
    188
Investors Group funds, 128,
    141, 142, 166, 177, 186

Jerome-Forget, Monique, 36

KPMG, 61

labour funds, 124, 149
Lagopoulos, Michael, 142
Lewis, Bea, 125
Life Underwriters of Canada,
    172
limited partnership, 183

Mackenzie funds, 141, 166, 186
marginal tax rate, 30, 57, 58
market index GICs, 76
Marketing Solutions, 169
Martin, Paul, 10, 14, 19, 27, 34,
    81, 95, 123, 149
maternity leave, 144
maturity ladders, 157
Mazankowski, Don, 95
McCallum, John, 140
McCracken, Mike, 14
McMaster University, 33
Mercedes Benz, 190
Midland Walwyn, 176
minimum annual payment,
    117–19
Money Concepts, 177
Moriarty, Kevin, 19
mortgage debt, 11, 22, 57
mortgage funds, 111
mortgage-backed securities, 171
mutual fund RRSPs, 76
mutual funds, 42, 59, 67, 81,
    171, 185

Nesbitt Burns, 114, 129, 158,
    176
no-load funds, 78

Office of the Superintendent of
    Financial Institutions, 32

Old Age Security, 10, 16, 88,
116, 134
O'Neill, Tim, 140
Ontario Coalition of Seniors,
125
Ontario Hydro, 82, 154
Ontario Ministry of Finance,
168
Ontario Savings Bonds, 153
Ontario Teachers' Pension Plan,
39
Organization for Economic Co-
operation and Development,
32, 34

Parizeau, Jacques, 82
Partners in Planning, 177
payroll deductions, 104
pension adjustment, 44, 52
pension income credit, 86
Peterson, Jim, 123
Pooley, Don, 175
power of attorney, 107
pre-authorized plan, 31
probate fees, 167
professional dues, 54

Quebec Pension Plan, 16
Quebec referendum, 48, 82, 140,
141, 165, 170

RBC Dominion Securities, 176
real assets, 67, 151
real estate, residential, 23, 32,
41, 71, 89, 139, 160, 164
redeemable GICs, 75
Regal Capital, 176
Registered Retirement Income
Funds (RRIFs), 26, 44, 88,
102, 109, 115

Registered Retirement Savings
Plans (RRSPs)
administration fees, 23
age limit, 25
basics, 43
carry forward, 20, 44, 98
contribution calculators, 55
contribution in kind, 98, 100,
137
contribution limits, 19, 52, 90
deadline, 45
eligible investments, 46
fees, 47
foreign content, 48, 79, 82
loans, 47, 106
mortgage, 90, 92
non-eligible investments, 46
overcontribution, 45, 107,
130, 135, 163
rebate, 42, 108
receipt, 29
season, 45, 30
self-directed, 78, 99, 130, 163
spousal, 85, 87, 134, 151
strategies, 126
swap assets, 22
taxation of, 121
transfers, 50, 78
rent controls, 68
rental income, 52, 109
rental losses, 54
retirement planning, 181
retiring allowance, 49
Revenue Canada, 24, 45, 83, 86,
92, 96, 107, 121, 132, 139,
181
Richards, Dan, 169
Richardson Greenshields, 176
risk, 74
Rodgers, Kelly, 14

Royal Bank, 82, 140, 141, 143, 185
Royal Trust, 23, 42, 142
Rubin, Jeff, 140

Sagit Investment, 186
Scarth, William, 33
scholarships, 54
Scotia Excelsior funds, 186
Scotia Investment Management, 9
ScotiaMcLeod, 176
Scudder Canada, 77, 186
self-employed, 29
Seniors Benefit, 10, 18, 34, 86, 116, 134, 158, 165
separation, 89
severance payment, 27, 49
sexual orientation, 87
small business, 85
social insurance, 53
source deductions, 133
spouse, 86
Standard and Poor's, 76, 146
Statistics Canada, 41, 129
Stiller, Calvin, 150
stock information, 184
stock markets, 72, 110, 146
stock quotes, 182
strip bonds, 74, 99, 101, 137, 152
subscription form, 192
systematic withdrawal plan, 166

Talvest Fund Management, 150, 186
tax credit, 46, 122
Tax Deduction Waiver, 29
tax planning, 181, 182
tax refund, 31
tax tables, 60

taxable income, 46
TD Evergreen, 176
Templeton funds, 69, 128, 141, 186
TIPS line, 53, 130
Today's Seniors, 117, 162
Toronto Dominion, 156, 177, 186
Toronto Stock Exchange, 76, 84, 128, 148, 160
Treasury bills, 155, 163
Trimark funds, 85, 128, 141, 166, 186
Tucillo, John, 152
20/20 funds, 128

underground economy, 57
union dues, 54
United States Labor Department, 11
United States National Association of Realtors, 152
universality, 34
University Avenue funds, 186
University of California, 33
user fees, 34

Wall Street Journal, 145, 175
website address, 180
will, 51, 167
William Mercer Ltd., 14, 17, 19, 125
withholding tax, 29, 30
Working Ventures, 149–50
World Bank, 34, 42, 83, 85

years in retirement, 9
Yorkton Securities, 176

zero coupon bonds, 154